7/6

D1587909

A drawing by Sickert

JOHN DAVIDSON

A Selection of his
POEMS

Preface by
T. S. ELIOT

Edited with an introduction by
MAURICE LINDSAY

With an essay by
HUGH McDIARMID

HUTCHINSON OF LONDON

HUTCHINSON & CO. *(Publishers)* LTD
178–202 Great Portland Street, London, W.1

London Melbourne Sydney
Auckland Bombay Toronto
Johannesburg New York

First published 1961

*This book has been set in Bembo type face. It has
been printed in Great Britain by The Anchor Press,
Ltd., in Tiptree, Essex, on Antique Wove paper and
bound by Taylor Garnett Evans & Co., Ltd., in
Watford, Herts*

ACKNOWLEDGEMENTS

I first became interested in John Davidson and his poetry in 1940, and since that time I have acquired almost a complete collection of his books, many of which are now comparatively rare. It was always my intention to bring out a comprehensive selection of his poems as soon as proved practicable after 1959, when the copyright on Davidson's poems expired and with it the prohibitive clause against re-publication in his eccentric Will. However, in 1957 Mr R. D. MacLeod produced a pamphlet in which he brought together most, but not quite all, of the things Davidson's contemporaries wrote about him. These, of course, must be regarded as primary documents by any future biographer, and, since they all come from published sources, are freely quoted here. Mr MacLeod also discovered in the British Museum a letter from Sir W. S. MacCormick to Edmund Gosse, the only document in the collection that I did not know about. I have made use of this document in my introductory essay.

I should like to thank the George Bernard Shaw trustees for permission to quote G.B.S.'s letter to me, written shortly before he died; Mr T. S. Eliot for his preface; Mr C. M. Grieve (Hugh McDiarmid) for his essay, 'John Davidson: Influences and Influence', which was written specially for this book. I should also like to thank the publishers of the various books from which I have quoted reminiscences of Davidson, including: J. J. Bell *I Remember* (Faber & Faber, Ltd, originally published by Porpoise Press); Frank Harris *Contemporary Portraits* (Methuen & Co. Ltd); Edgar Jepson *Memories of a Victorian* (Victor Gollancz Ltd); Neil Munro *The Brave Days* (Faber & Faber, Ltd); Ernest Rhys *Everyman Remembers* (J. M. Dent & Sons Ltd); Grant Richards *Author Hunting* (Richards Press Ltd); Priscilla Thouless *Modern Poetic Drama* (Basil Blackwell); and W. B. Yeats *Autobiographies* (Mrs W. B. Yeats and Macmillan of London and New York).

Contents

Preface

T. S. ELIOT

I feel a peculiar reverence, and acknowledge a particular debt, towards poets whose work impressed me deeply in my formative years between the ages of sixteen and twenty. Some were of an earlier age—the late sixteenth and early seventeenth centuries—some of another language; and of these, two were Scots: the author of *The City of Dreadful Night*, and the author of *Thirty Bob a Week*. It is because I am given an opportunity of expressing, once again, my gratitude to John Davidson, that I write this preface.

I have, indeed, no other excuse. Mr Maurice Lindsay has provided the biographical account needed to introduce the work of John Davidson, and Mr Hugh McDiarmid has written at length of Davidson and of Davidson's significance in his own development. I cannot better the testimony of a fellow makar of Davidson. Modesty requires me to write briefly; but loyalty requires me to write.

What exactly is my debt to John Davidson I cannot tell, any more than I can describe the nature of my debt to James Thomson: I only know that the two debts differ from each other. Some may think, from what I have said on this subject before (Mr Lindsay has quoted my word which appeared in *The Saltire Review*), that the obligation to Davidson was merely for technical hints. Certainly, *Thirty Bob a Week* seems to me the only poem in which Davidson freed himself completely from the poetic diction of English verse of his time (just as *Non Sum Qualis Eram* seems to me the one poem in which, by a slight shift of rhythm, Ernest Dowson freed himself). But I am sure that I found inspiration in the content of the poem, and in the complete fitness of content and idiom: for I also had a good many dingy urban images to reveal. Davidson had a great theme, and also found an idiom which elicited the greatness of the theme, which endowed this thirty-bob-a-week clerk with a dignity that would not have appeared if a more conventional poetic diction had been employed. The personage that Davidson created in this poem has haunted me all my life, and the poem is to me a great poem for ever.

I do not wish, however, to give the impression that for me Davidson is the author of one poem only. Davidson wrote too much and sometimes tediously; and I am happy with this selection. Here are some lovely lyrics and ballads; *The Runnable Stag* has run in my head for a good many years now; and I have a fellow feeling with the poet who could look with a poet's eye on the Isle of Dogs and Millwall Dock. To me, Davidson's blank verse is rather hard going. I allow for the fact that, as in the case of Thomas Hardy, I find the philosophy uncongenial. No matter: in everything that Davidson wrote I recognize a real man, to be treated not only with respect but with homage.

T. S. Eliot

Introduction

MAURICE LINDSAY

I

'MANKIND has cast me out.' So begins John Davidson's 'The Testament of a Man Forbid', which, like so many of his poems, contains a good deal of autobiographical truth.

John Davidson was born in Barrhead, Renfrewshire, on 11th April 1857 the son of Alexander Davidson, a minister of the Evangelical Union. Before young Davidson's first birthday, his father had been transferred to Greenock; and it was of Greenock[1] that John Davidson later wrote affectionately in his 'Ballad in Blank Verse of the Making of a Poet':

> . . . this grey town
> That pipes the morning up before the lark
> With shrieking steam, and from a hundred stalks
> Lacquers the sooty sky; where hammers clang
> On iron hulls, and cranes in harbours creak
> Rattle and swing, whole cargoes on their necks;
> Where men sweat gold that others hoard or spend,
> And lurk like vermin in their narrow streets:
> This old grey town, this firth, the further strand
> Spangled with hamlets, and the wooded steeps,
> Whose rocky tops behind each other press,
> Fantastically carved like antique helms
> High-hung in heaven's cloudy armoury,
> Is world enough for me.

[1] In an interview for the *Bookman* which Davidson gave Jane T. Stoddart in 1895, the poet said: 'When I am alone and not preoccupied, the sweep of the coast between Helensburgh and Loch Long comes before me, and however far I may travel in the future, no other coast can be so deeply graven on my memory.'

But the grim, grey, pious atmosphere of the busy Clyde seaport did not long remain 'world enough for' him. He was later to refer in a letter to '. . . the Philistinism, in which I was brought up, and which is both the nitrogen and the oxygen of Greenock'. It has sometimes been stated that the teachings of the Evangelical Union were neither Calvinistic nor unliberal. Davidson, who had to endure them, apparently thought differently. He rebelled not only against his father's teaching, but against Christianity itself. In his 'Ballad in Blank Verse' Davidson describes how his unbelief broke his mother's heart. The poem also reveals an attitude of harsh condemnation towards his father, an attitude which bursts out again in 'A Woman and her Son'.

Davidson left the Highlanders' Academy in Greenock when he was thirteen and went to work in the chemical laboratory of Walker's Sugar Refinery. The following year he became assistant to the Public Analyst of Greenock. No doubt it was these two years of experience that fostered what was to be a lifelong interest in science.

In 1872 however, he went back to the Highlanders' Academy, this time as a pupil-teacher. He spent the winter of 1876–7 as an arts student at Edinburgh University, where his studies included Latin and Greek, but he seems to have stayed only one year at the University, for after teaching during the autumn of 1877 at Alexander's Charity School, Glasgow, he became a master at Perth Academy early in the new year. There he remained for three years, moving to Kelvinside Academy, Glasgow, in 1881. Two years later he was teaching in Hutchinson's Charity School at Paisley.

Then in 1884 he temporarily abandoned schoolmastering and became a clerk in the Glasgow office of Clark's Thread Mill. However much teaching may have irked his impetuous spirit, copying figures into ledgers proved more tedious still, and in 1885 he again became a teacher, this time in Morrison's Academy at Crieff. There he remained for three more years, finishing his teaching career in 1889 as a master in a small private school at Greenock.

One of his fellow masters at Kelvinside Academy, D. H.

Louden, has left us a description of Davidson when the poet was about twenty-three:

Forty-seven years ago an angel came slowly along the Great Western Road, but his passage aroused no particular interest, for he looked like a schoolmaster, and that is not what the public expect in a visitor from on high. Trading on his outward seeming, he applied for a post at Kelvinside Academy, and the name he gave, John Davidson, was in itself a testimonial of solid, stolid integrity and worth. The unsuspecting Head appointed him forthwith and he was presently to be seen moving about corridor and classroom more or less like an ordinary mortal.

To the boys he seemed, as one of them has left on record, a badly shaped, untidily dressed little man with a brown beard. He never looked happy or comfortable; probably he felt out of his element. In his class he was known as 'Jenny Wren'.

Mr J. J. Bell, another of his pupils, says that the beard gave the boys 'The idea of a person of ripe age, when he must still have been under thirty.' Moreover, he inclined to baldness, and a high forehead rose above a pair of bright dark eyes. 'We named him "Jenny Wren" and "Cocky", nay, more—and it shames me to record the fact—we dubbed him "Cockabendy". Whether he was a successful teacher as one judged by "results" I cannot say.
. . . We had not then heard that he himself "wrote poetry", but the knowledge that he was a poet would not have moved us, except to merriment, or, perchance, mockery. . . .'

J. J. Bell, who achieved some fame in his own lifetime with his impish urchin *Wee MacGregor*, also passed from Kelvinside Academy to Morrison's Academy in Crieff, so, once again, had Davidson as a master. In his autobiography *I Remember* Bell recalled Davidson's teaching career when it was almost at an end:

. . . the English master was a small, dark man with a very bald head, short beard, bright eyes and bird-like manner. It was not my first acquaintance with him, for he had come to Crieff from Kelvinside Academy, my earlier school. His name was John Davidson. I am not going to tell his nick-name. His is too tragic a memory. He was not successful as a teacher, though he strove earnestly to instil in us a regard for the great authors, and did succeed in impressing some of us by his recitations from Shakespeare's plays. His heart was in that part of his work, not in the dreariness of parsing, analysis and so forth. At that time we did not suspect him of being a poet, nor of writing anything, except lessons on the blackboard and comments on our exercises.

A year or so later he published, in Glasgow, a novel, or novelette, called *The North Wall*, price one shilling. One night, in the Christmas or Easter holidays, my father brought home a copy, and my brother and I were astonished at such a thing coming out of our schoolmaster; not that we thought much of the story itself, which was, of course, beyond our youthful intelligence. But one night—how it came about I do not know—my father brought Mr Davidson himself to the house, and for the time being, at least, he was not a schoolmaster to us; and when, on returning to Crieff, we discovered that none of our fellows knew about *The North Wall*, we were inclined to give ourselves airs. Before long the novel was followed by two plays—*Bruce, a Drama*, and *Smith, a Tragedy*—and the author abandoned teaching to shoulder a heavier, if less irksome, burden. He and his wife[1]—he married while at Crieff—must have endured hard times, but with the coming of the 'nineties it did look as though the reward were at hand.

The idea of abandoning teaching for a literary career had probably been in Davidson's mind for many years. Just before he went to Perth, Davidson met Swinburne at a reception in the Glasgow home of Professor John Nichol, the first occupant of the Chair of English literature at Glasgow University. According to Gosse, the twenty-one-year-old Davidson read to Swinburne some youthful verses, whereupon Swinburne supposedly put his hands on the younger man's head and said, 'Poet!' This was a romantic gesture, supposing it ever to have been made, which Swinburne possibly 'borrowed' from the banker poet Samuel Rogers, whose sanctimonious verses once won him a considerable, if short-lived, reputation. With his hand on the boy Swinburne's head, Rogers had said, 'I prophesy that you will be a poet, too!' the last word of his prophecy not then possessing the ironic twist that the judgment of posterity has given it.

The meeting with Swinburne fired Davidson's ambitions. On 28th March 1878 the younger man addressed the first of two youthfully arrogant letters to 'The Nightingale of Poets', enclosing some of his own verses 'with every good wish from a

[1] Annie Smith.

4

singing bird of some description, and probable quality'. Davidson explained to Swinburne that he had given up his job as a teacher, and asked that, if his poems were thought to have merit, Swinburne should try to find a publisher for them. Davidson added:

> If I am what I take myself to be, my opinion carries great weight. . . . I send them to you because I have seen you, because you did not patronize me, because I can trust you, because I take you to be not only the greatest poet since Shakespeare, but also the greatest writer as he was likewise before you.

Not surprisingly, Swinburne, who in any case was in ill-health at this time, did not answer this importunate letter. Two months later Davidson wrote again, asking Swinburne to destroy the first letter and assuring the English poet that he was 'ready and had been any day since I began your works to lay my neck beneath your foot and call you king'. This letter, like the first, remained unanswered. Although Davidson never lost his admiration for Swinburne, the complete lack of encouragement which his brash approach had met with may have made it seem prudent not to abandon the teaching profession for the time being.

Towards the close of 1889 Davidson finally gave up schoolteaching and followed his friend John Nichol, who had retired to London. There, Davidson was befriended by, among others, the publisher John Lane, and he became one of the few regular Scottish contributors to *The Yellow Book*. At first, while 'the bloom was on', things went well for Davidson; two sons had been born; his reputation, based on his early lyrical poems, his ballads, and his eclogues, was steadily growing. Though he can never have been affluent, he was able to enjoy London club life. The kind of poverty with which he had to live in his later years had not yet caught up with him, and he had not yet openly declared his quarrel with mankind.

Soon he was on friendly terms with many of London's most celebrated literary figures of the 'nineties. The flamboyant Frank Harris, in his *Contemporary Portraits*, put down his impressions of Davidson soon after the Scottish poet had settled in London:

It was in 1889 that I first met John Davidson. . . . He was a little below middle height, but strongly built with square shoulders and remarkably fine face and head: the features were almost classically regular, the eyes dark brown and large, the forehead high, the hair and moustache black. His manners were perfectly frank and natural: he met every one in the same unaffected kindly human way: I never saw a trace in him of snobbishness or incivility. Possibly a great man, I said to myself, certainly a man of genius, for simplicity of manner alone is in England almost a proof of extraordinary endowment. . . . I took him to a house at Wimbledon where his poetry was already known and loved. As soon as Davidson found he was among friends and admirers who could appreciate his work, he let himself go with the ingenuousness of a boy. He recited passages that he liked in his own work or the work of others, and, of course, one noticed immediately that he had an extraordinary knowledge of the best English poetry. Like most poets, he chanted his lines, marking the metre of the verse a little too distinctly; but there was a certain impressiveness in the peculiarity. . . . It was his sincerity which struck me most at the outset; three or four years later he showed me that his unswerving loyalty to truth was an even deeper characteristic and had brought him to many-sided wisdom. He saw his own people with the unflinching direct vision which Dante turned on his Florentines. . . . It should be impossible for me to talk of Davidson without insisting again and again on the charm of his companionship. His whimsicalities of judgment were really proof of his chivalric earnestness. If he had thought that Henley had been ill-used by the world, or if he had felt that Henley had given great work or much love to the world, nothing would have induced him to say a word against him. His thirst was for justice: he was always trying to establish the equitable balance: James Thomson had been neglected, therefore he overpraised James Thomson. Meredith was passing through his day almost unnoticed. Davidson never let his name go by without the warmest praise. And this chivalry of disposition went with a sweet temper, and the most generous appreciation of his friends and of contemporary work. . . .

In the red-plush days of the 'nineties Davidson was mainly concerned with trying to find a new means of handling the romantic forms and ideas of his Victorian predecessors. Often he failed. Sometimes his ear let him down; sometimes his images went soft. His textures frequently reveal odd bare patches, which suggest insufficient revision. But now and again, when he allowed his lyrical impulse and his descriptive faculties to remain

untrammelled by self-conscious poeticism, as in 'Romney Marsh',
he succeeded.

> Masts in the offing wagged their tops;
> The swinging waves pealed on the shore;
> The saffron beach, all diamond drops
> And beads of surge, prolonged the roar . . .

In later life Davidson came to despise the mass of mankind
because, in his view, its members so completely failed to realize
their potentialities. During the first half of the 'nineties, however,
he had considerable sympathy with the poverty in which the
working classes of London were enveloped; a poverty the
Scottish counterpart of which he had been familiar with at
Greenock as a boy. This sympathy led him to study their speech,
and adapt it for the purposes of poetry. Sometimes he tried
grafting the colloquial idiom on to the high-flown artificial con-
ventions of the English *Yellow Book* poets. The result of these
experiments was as disastrous as the attempt of Burns a century
earlier to blend the peasant Scots idiom of agrarian Ayrshire and
the mannerisms of Augustan England. Occasionally, however,
Davidson managed to forget the literary fashions of the day, and
the result could be a splendid poem, like 'Thirty Bob a Week',
which rings wholly true.

> I couldn't touch a stop and turn a screw,
> And set the blooming world a-work for me,
> Like such as cut their teeth—I hope, like you—
> On the handle of a skeleton gold key;
> I cut mine on a leek, which I eat it every week:
> I'm a clerk at thirty bob as you can see.
>
> But I don't allow it's luck and all a toss;
> There's no such thing as being starred and crossed;
> It's just the power of some to be a boss,
> And the bally power of others to be bossed:
> I face the music, sir; you bet I ain't a cur;
> Strike me lucky if I don't believe I'm lost! . . .

The plight of the clerk's family is realistically described, with

7

much emphasis on courage in the face of adversity, an attitude which Davidson insisted upon even to the manner of his own dying. The rebel Davidson, who was so soon to refuse to accept the ordered scheme of things, reveals his inner self in another stanza.

> I step into my heart and there I meet
> A god-almighty devil singing small,
> Who would like to shout and whistle in the street,
> And squelch the passers flat against the wall;
> If the whole world was a cake he had the power to take,
> He would take it, ask for more, and eat them all. . . .

'Thirty Bob a Week', his third *Yellow Book* poem, has a sincerity and a dignity which, in my view, puts it far above the poems by Rudyard Kipling with which it most obviously invites comparison. It reflects not only Davidson's admiration for the man who is self-reliant and courageous no matter how heavy the odds against him, but also the beginnings of the personal belief which Davidson substituted for Evangelical Christianity, and which later obsessed him: the belief that Man is the Universe made conscious.

But 'Thirty Bob a Week' is not only a fine poem in its own right; it has had a considerable influence upon, among others, T. S. Eliot, as Mr Eliot announced in a recorded tribute for radio which celebrated the centenary of Davidson's birth.

'I read John Davidson's poems first,' Mr Eliot said. 'I can't remember whether it was towards the end of my school days or in my first year or two at Harvard University. But I read them at a time when I was reading the poets of the 'nineties, who were the only poets—most of them were dead, of course—who at that period of history seemed to have anything to offer to me as a beginner. What I wanted, I think, from the poets of the 'nineties was what they did not have in common with the Pre-Raphaelites, but what was new and original in their work. And I remember three poets in particular. One was Arthur Symons, some of his poems; another was Ernest Dowson, again one or two poems; and the third was Davidson, in his "Thirty Bob a Week". From these men I got the idea that one could write poetry in an English such as one would speak oneself. A colloquial idiom. There was a spoken rhythm in some of their poems. Now, I admire other poems of Davidson very much indeed. I think they should be read again and again; but it is "Thirty Bob a Week" which made a terrific impact on me. And with some of those by the other men I have mentioned, I think it prepared me for initiation into the work of some of the French symbolists, such as Laforgue, whom I came across shortly after. But "Thirty Bob a Week" has a very important place in the development of my own poetic technique.'

It was the Davidson of the early 'nineties who influenced T. S. Eliot. By the middle of the 'nineties, Davidson was beginning to find it more difficult to earn his living. Although according to Yeats Davidson boasted that his agent 'now gets me forty pounds a ballad, and I made three hundred pounds out of my last book of verse',[1] the poet whom Edgar Jepson, in *Memories of a Victorian*, remembered 'in his short beard, silk hat and morning coat' as resembling 'a commercial traveller at loggerheads with the world', could not adapt himself easily to journalism. He read for John Lane and Elkin Mathews, the directors of the Bodley Head press. But in June 1894 he was already complaining to Lane that his average income from all sources was only thirty-five shillings a week, and that he found himself unable to do the work he wanted because of shortage of money, a situation which not even his wife's economy could alleviate. He faced up to these economic difficulties with an outward display of gusto which brought him into conflict with Yeats. The initial cause of the friction between the two poets is not now known, but in September 1892, after an adverse review of *The Countess Cathleen* had appeared in the *Daily Chronicle*, Yeats's father, Jack B. Yeats, said in a letter to his son:

Who could have written the *D. Chronicle* criticism? Was it Davidson —as a *tit* for your *tat*? The tats were provoking and rather unnecessary and since probably totally unexpected therefore the more bewildering and enraging to the fiery Scot. . . . The criticism was a very effective

[1] *Ballads and Songs.*

piece of coarse journalism, but by its nature only appealed to the merest vulgar and [is] not likely to do you or anybody any harm. . . .

I laughed very much and without any bitterness over the offending criticism and assuming Davidson to be the author liked him all the better. It is a good sign when a man does not know how to wound.

Obviously Yeats and Davidson were temperamentally so different that the one could hardly have failed to irritate the other. But it would seem from Jack B. Yeats's letter that it was the Irish poet who opened hostilities.

In his *Autobiographies* Yeats described the disrupting effect which Davidson had on the Rhymers' Club:

He saw in delicate, laborious, discriminating taste an effeminate pedantry, and would, when that mood was on him, delight in all that seemed healthy, popular, and bustling. Once when I had praised Herbert Horne for his knowledge and his taste, he burst out, 'if a man must be a connoisseur, let him be a connoisseur in women'. He, indeed, was accustomed, in the most characteristic phrase of his type, to describe the Rhymers as lacking in 'blood and guts', and very nearly brought us to an end by attempting to supply the deficiency by the addition of four Scotsmen. He brought all four upon the same evening, and one read out a poem upon the Life-boat, evidently intended for a recitation; another described how, when gold-digging in Australia, he had fought and knocked down another miner for doubting the rotundity of the earth; while of the remainder I can remember nothing except that they excelled in argument. He insisted upon their immediate election, and the Rhymers, through that complacency of good manners whereby educated Englishmen so often surprise me, obeyed, though secretly resolved never to meet again; and it cost me seven hours' work to get another meeting, and vote the Scotsmen out. A few days later I chanced upon Davidson at some restaurant; he was full of amiability, and when we parted shook my hand, and proclaimed enthusiastically that I had 'blood and guts'. I think he might have grown to be a successful man had he been enthusiastic instead about Dowson or Johnson, or Horne or Symons, for they had what I still lacked, conscious deliberate craft, and what I must lack always, scholarship. They had taught me that violent energy, which is like a fire of straw, consumes in a few minutes the nervous vitality, and is useless in the arts. Our fire must burn slowly, and we must constantly turn away to think, constantly analyse what we have done, be content even to have a little life outside our work, to show, perhaps, to other men, as little as the watch-mender shows, his magnifying-glass caught in his screwed-up eye. Only then do we learn to conserve our vitality, to keep our mind enough under control and to make our technique sufficiently flexible for expression of the emotions of life as they arise. A few months after our meeting in the Museum, Davidson had spent his inspiration. 'The fires are out,' he said, 'and I must hammer the cold iron.'

The Rhymers' Club met at the Old Cheshire Cheese, and in his autobiography, *Everyman Remembers*, Ernest Rhys recorded what seems a reasonably objective view of the relationship between Davidson and Yeats:

One frequent attendant at the Cheshire Cheese was the author of *Fleet Street Eclogues*, John Davidson; but he refused to become an out-and-out member, saying he did not care to be ranked as one of a coterie. There was in him a strain of angry pride, fostered in him by his hard life and his want of recognition, not so much from the London critics as from the big public which ought to buy one's books. Also there is such a thing as artistic jealousy, and a touch of it, added perhaps to another touch of temperamental incompatibility, had given John Davidson a lurking dislike to some members of the club. Of these Yeats was his pet aversion.

Rhys also recalls how one night D. H. Lawrence, Ford Madox Ford, Yeats and Ezra Pound assembled at his home for an informal poetry reading:

Davidson came—very late, and refused point-blank to contribute his quota. However, after some persuasion, he read us his *In Romney Marsh*, which had a great ring in it. . . .

That obstinate prickliness in his nature, which grew more barbed as time went on, struck even so sympathetic a friend as Richard Le Gallienne, who first interested Lane in Davidson, and managed to find some good in *Earl Lavender*, possibly the poor best of Davidson's appallingly bad society novels.[1]

In his gracefully written recollection of *The Romantic 'Nineties*, Le Gallienne said of Davidson:

[1] For a survey of Davidson's novels, see 'John Davidson: The Novels of a Poet', by P. Turner; *Cambridge Journal*, Vol. 5, 1952.

My intimacy with him covered only the years of transient bright-
ness when, after a long grind at schoolmastering in Scotland, he came
up to London in 1890, definitely to embrace a literary career. He had
already published one or two plays without success, particularly his
brilliant fantastic pantomime *Scaramouch in Naxos*, as well as a remarkable prose romance *Perfervid*, both of which ought to be republished,
and in 1891 he published a volume of poems called *In a Music Hall*,
which made the critics aware of him, paving the way for the enthusiastic reception in 1893 of his *Fleet Street Eclogues*, which I had the
honour of accepting for Lane. It was through this book that I came to
know him, and his recognition of such service as I was able to do him
in the newspapers was as generous and wholehearted as it was unusual.
I remember with gratitude that when there was a concerted attack
upon me and my 'log-rolling' propensities,[1] which lasted no less than a
fortnight in the *Westminster Gazette*—to me a joyous and exhilarating
all-in-the-day's work experience—Davidson stood manfully by me. . . .

And again:

Someone has said the 'nineties was a time of 'little giants'. The
expression is a good one, and the man whom perhaps it especially fits
was John Davidson, whose personality was rocky and stubborn and
full of Scotch fight, with no little of Scotch pig-headedness. But with
him, as with the lion in Holy Writ, within whose jaws the wild bees
built their honeycombs, it was a case of *ex forte dulcedo*: for beneath his
proud, rather pragmatic exterior, and that Highland manner which
brings a suggestion of always going armed against offence, his nature
was full of human kindness and repressed tenderness. His life was hard
from boyhood, and even when recognition of his gifts came to him,
he continued, at least, to regard it as hard, because he found, as many
another poet has done, that fame was more cry than wool, and that
earning his livelihood continued as difficult as ever. In this he was really
no worse off than several of his famous contemporaries, but he had
no bend in him, would not, or could not, stoop to journalism. A poet
who insisted on reality in his work, he was incapable of adapting
himself to those materialistic conditions with which the most inspired
poet must compromise if he is to continue to exist.

Davidson's name had been canvassed for the Poet Laureateship

[1] A critic in the *Westminster Gazette* attacked Le Gallienne for naming six new major
poets in a review of poetry for 1894. The list included two, Gale and Hayes, who came
to nothing: but the others were Symons, Francis Thompson, Yeats and Davidson. 'Roll
thou my log and I will roll thee thine,' quipped Ricardo Stephens of Le Gallienne, in his
'Ballade of the Poets'.

when it became vacant in 1895 upon the death of Lord Tennyson. He himself considered that Swinburne was the only poet worthy of the office, then held in higher regard than possibly it is now. In any case, the Laureateship went to Alfred Austin. By this time Davidson's financial circumstances were becoming desperate. Aid came to him from an unexpected quarter.

In 1957 R. D. MacLeod discovered in the British Museum a letter about Davidson's circumstances written by Sir W. S. McCormick to Edmund Gosse on 6th December 1898. McCormick, who had known Davidson since about 1878, had been a lecturer under Professor Nichol in Glasgow in 1884 before becoming Professor of English at St Andrew's University, and later still a distinguished University Administrator, the first Secretary of the Carnegie Trust for the Universities, and one of the original trustees of the Carnegie United Kingdom Trust. Clearly, McCormick was exactly the kind of influential public figure to whom Gosse would turn for help in procuring a pension for an impoverished man of letters. Gosse's original letter has not been preserved, but from McCormick's answer, we may guess at its contents:

... *Why* is he so poor?—First, his poetry, as is natural, hasn't given him a living wage. He has managed to produce, say, *one* volume a year. When he was boomed, this may have given him £100, perhaps, a year—though possibly not as much. Now, when the boom (& bloom) is over, I don't suppose he gets more than £50. As to other work, as reviewing, he is practically unfitted for it. For one thing, he is too self-centred: then he writes with difficulty—very slowly— perhaps too conscientiously. He doesn't get any *regular* work at it— and his spasmodic efforts at it cannot bring him in much. But between the two he has managed by strict economy to make two ends meet till this last year, when his 3 or 4 months illness laid him hors de combat. He lived down in some village Brighton-way, for the past few years— out of London for cheapness' sake. And as far as I can make out the solitary life, and financial anxieties together preyed on his nerves: and, as I could make out from his wife, he was very seriously ill—forbidden by the doctor to do any work for months—and seems even to have been bedridden for a considerable part of that time. But the memory of it seems to be so horrible to him, that he felt disinclined to talk of it, or to give me any details. This period of making no income, together with the added expence of doctors' bills (his poor wife was herself ill, during a part of his illness) must have been a terribly serious drain on any slender means they had, or rather, as I guess, it handicapped the future by debt, which any work he has been able to do since has no doubt been needed to pay off. Then as to his success with *Pour la Couronne*,[1] I do not think his royalties exceed £150 or so. It was his first experience with theatrical managers: & I remember his telling me that Robertson's manager (not Robertson) had not treated him fairly or even justly in the matter.

So much for income. As to expenditure, besides his wife and two boys, he had up till last year or the year before (I forget which) when his mother died, a mother & sister in Edinburgh to help, as far as his scant means allowed. They made some scanty income by letting lodgings to students in Edgh. Univy, [sic]—but not enough to live on. So I think Davidson tried to send them enough to pay the rent of their house but he wasn't always able to do this. Now his sister is carrying it on alone: whether he has been able to help her since her mother's death I don't know. I shouldn't think so. But for six months or so after, she came to live with him, which must have been so far an additional drain.

There is yet a more serious tragedy in poor D.'s life which I think I ought not to omit, and which I leave to your discretion to give to your Council, or not, as you see fit. I got in confidence from him—indeed, I *had* to know as I was giving him some assistance in the matter at the time. And as I understand any information received by your Committee is absolutely *private*, I feel I must give it in order to state his case fully.

There is insanity in his family. His only brother was in an asylum for some years. I think it was five or six years ago (perhaps more) that the first symptoms broke out, although before that he was quite incapacitated for working for his living, and was living with, and supported by, his mother and sister in Edinburgh. Ultimately it came to a crisis. The brother tried to kill the mother with a carving knife which he had secreted under his bed. (Knowing of his murderous lunacy they had for months been careful to keep from him all sharp instruments—and had to be continually on the watch.) In connection with this matter poor Davidson had to make many journeys to Edinburgh: the lodgings of his mother and sister were naturally

---

[1] Davidson's only theatrical success was his translation of Coppée's play, which was staged at the Lyceum with Mrs. Pat Campbell in the cast. She adored his Scots accent and his 'grave manner', and produced his blank verse translation of Hugo's *Ruy Blas* in 1904. But the critics found that it made better reading than theatre, and it ran for only a fortnight. Nevertheless, she commissioned him to translate Racine's *Phèdre*, but this was neither produced nor published. Priscilla Thouless's *Modern Poetic Drama* (1934) contains a detailed study of Davidson's plays.

14

avoided for a time by the students: and he had further serious expences in getting his brother placed in an asylum. About eighteen months ago the brother came out of the asylum. Davidson had to arrange with him that he should go to Australia, had to provide funds for his going there, & send him some sum (I don't know how much) to start him on his arrival.

I need not point out how—apart from the additional expences incurred—this terrible strain on him must have affected his power of working & of money-making. It was at this period of despair, indeed, that D. first allowed me to help him a little—apart from some small assistance I had got for him at his first start in London, for which I was partly responsible. . . .

It was at this time of D.'s sore affliction that I had my best opportunity of seeing to the bottom of D.'s character and of his brave strong heart. Circumstances that would have overwhelmed most men were with him an incentive to still more strenuous effort. And I fancy that it has been the over-tension of that strain that ultimately reacted in the collapse of nerves and physique early this year. I admit that it left traces of morbidness in his work—e.g. in parts of his *Second Fleet Street Eclogues*, & in some of his autobiographical poetry, as *The Making of a Poet*, etc. How could it be otherwise? But I believe—in both from what I have seen of his poetry and of himself lately—that he has come through it unscathed—has worked out his mental and spiritual salvation—with his character and his poetry the richer and fuller for what he has experienced. Please note that any figures I give as to D.'s possible sources of income are mere guesses. The absolute facts could be got only by asking D. himself. But one point I know for certain, which I see I have omitted. In the case of *every* volume, he had to obtain, by the kindness of his publisher, an advance of a considerable part of the probable proceeds long before its publication, and has therefore never been able to pull himself out of the miserable condition of having to live upon what he had not yet earned. . . .

On this last point, Davidson's later publisher, Grant Richards, in his amusing autobiography *Author Hunting*, recorded that with him

. . . only two of Davidson's books covered the out-of-pocket expenses of their production: out of *Fleet Street and other Poems* I made about fifteen pounds, and out of *Holiday* twenty—in each case without reckoning anything for office expenses.

How much money came to Davidson as a result of the

collaboration between McCormick and Gosse and their friends we do not know. But in a letter written in December 1898, and conjectured by R. D. MacLeod to have been addressed to McCormick, Davidson's gratitude overflowed:

This very extraordinary event, great jail-delivery of despair and temporary installation in the seventh heavens has taken place. I am unable as yet to connect it with any name. It is the entirely magical operation of a great unknown and unknowable entity, a Fund. . . .
It is quite true as I said before that we are sliding down an icefloe, tilted at an angle of forty-five degrees, at a frightful rate of acceleration; the ice was catching fire with the friction and the gulf yawned and sucked its tongue and licked its boltered chops almost within snapping distance. Hey, presto! The Fund claps its fundament on the other end of the floe; we are hoisted to equilibrium, snatched up, and planted once more on *terra firma*, and we haven't found our feet or our heads yet.

A further reason for his being on the icefloe—a decline in his poetic popularity—was the change in his literary style and outlook which occurred about the turn of the century. He grew tired of the imitation ballads and artificial eclogues that were so much to the taste of the public. The hard-pressed poet whom Yeats thought lacking in 'pose and gesture' spent the last years of his life writing a series of Plays and Testaments, saying what he wanted to say regardless of the cost to himself.

In those works of his last years, he sought to pull down the religious culture of the past, and build a new culture, based on science and on his conviction, inspired by Nietzsche, that Man must rejoice in being, because, made up of the same ingredients as the Universe, he is, in fact, the Universe made conscious, and therefore inherently a creature of greatness.

As he became more deeply absorbed in Nietzschean philosophy, he retreated further and further into angry isolation. Frank Harris, who had lost touch with Davidson in the middle 'nineties, met him again in 1903 or 1904, and found him changed:

He had grown self-assertive, and at the same time had developed a certain bitterness of attitude which seemed out of tune with his kindly temperament and fair habit of mind. . . . When he was about forty years of age Davidson came to this pass: starting from near the bottom of society he had won to the very top: he had made a name as common as Smith immortal; had crowned himself in the Temple not made with hands, eternal in the Heavens, and yet he was confronted with the vast indifference of the public that cares less for poets than for acrobats, and exposed to the envious attacks of venomous poetasters and journalists, and this at a time when he was without money and without influence, but with health failing and disease threatening. It is to Davidson's honour that in that dread hour he never whimpered or whined or thought of giving in; instead of abating his high pretensions as a poet, he set them higher still; he would be a prophet as well, or rather he was a prophet, and what was true to him, that he would set forth with all emphasis. Alas! in spite of his sincerity and unswerving devotion to truth, in spite of all his gifts as a singer, and all his goodness as lover and father and friend, he could discover no light in the darkness, neither sun nor star. But his courage held; he would sing all-encompassing Night, then, and Nothingness, and himself set therein sightless yet a god! the only god, indeed! That way madness lies: for pride dwarfs the mind and maims the soul. . . . Every time we met from 1907 onwards there was deterioration in him: the worse he did, the higher he put his claims, and there was nothing to be done for him or with him. If one praised his poetry and begged him to give the world more of it, he pooh-poohed it all. I reminded him once of how exquisitely he had written of larks and their singing, and he replied: 'My dear Frank, Shelley did it better, and I have better things to do, greater songs to sing; which you will not listen to.'

It is now quite clear that it was Davidson who was right and Harris, the upholder of the easy, popular view, who was wrong.

In 1906 Davidson was given a Civil List Pension of £100 a year; but by then, this was too little to steady his position. Nevertheless, he continued to make a brave flourish. Grant Richards recorded that Davidson's pension was paid quarterly:

and on the day on which he received it he would ask either Beerbohm or me to dinner. He asked us in turn. The invited guest would arrive at the Grosvenor Club at the corner of Dover Street, Piccadilly, and having been given a glass of sherry he would be taken, on foot if it were fine, in a cab if it were wet, to the Trocadero, where a table would be waiting the poet's arrival and where he had already indicated that

17

he was to be served with neither the five-shilling nor the seven-and-sixpenny meal, but with the best, which cost half a guinea. A bottle of very good, almost superlative, claret would be the wine, and after dinner would be coffee and old brandy—not the most expensive of cognacs, not that one whose price per glass would indecently affront a guest (for it was the Trocadero habit to have the wine waiter stick in front of you the several bottles, each bearing a large and priced label), but one which would properly complete the meal of which we had partaken. Then we would smoke lavish cigars from the cabinet of the Grosvenor Club, for even on this day of the nation's quarterly appreciation of his worth, Davidson retained respect for the shillings in his pocket and he knew that a club cigar would cost less than those supplied by the restaurant's head-waiter.

There in the Trocadero we would sit and talk. Davidson would mellow, would cast off all doubts as to the future, would be certain of a great success, and he would give you the feeling that for the moment he loved the world for your sake. And indeed those evenings were the occasions when the world became attractive in his eyes, rosy —and that not because his stomach lusted after rich food and good wine but because they were for the moment the symbols, the outward signs, of the comfort, the luxury, he knew to be his due. That meal, four times a year, at the Trocadero, was his one concession to extravagance. But at a certain hour the clock would strike. He knew too well the time at which the last train would leave Victoria for Streatham and when it approached nothing would induce him to linger. No: he would take his hat and his stick from the cloakroom attendant and, thanking you for the pleasure your company had given him, he would summon a hansom, tip the commissionaire and rattle away down Piccadilly.

About this time, a fellow Scot found himself faced with the task of having to call upon Davidson on behalf of some of the citizens of Greenock. The Greenock connection may partly have been responsible for the savageness of the reception which the envoy got, and which Neil Munro described in *The Brave Days*:

For 1907 Greenock decided to have John Davidson, the poet, for 'The Immortal Memory'. It was felt that he, at least, would not disappoint them. But to clinch the matter, an ex-secretary of the Club who was leaving for France undertook to tackle Davidson personally on his way through London. This gentleman, like Davidson himself, had been, for years, a school teacher in Greenock; was an almost fanatical admirer of the poet's work, and had by lectures to Literary Societies made it almost as familiar to the Clyde and the West Coast as the work of Burns himself.

Some time before, the poet had contributed a charming series of prose articles to a Glasgow newspaper under the general title of 'Random Itinerary', and they had abruptly ceased. The Editor[1] (who was also editor of a Life and Works of Burns), learning of the embassy to Davidson on behalf of the Greenock Burns Club, asked the ambassador, at the same time, to let the poet know there was a great demand in the West of Scotland for a continuation of the 'Random Itinerary'. All attempts to stir Mr Davidson up by letter had failed.

In due course, the ambassador reported upon his mission as follows: 'He lives an infernally long way out; I had to take two trains to reach his suburb, and then walk about two miles to get to his house. It was one of a long row of neat-looking but obviously cheap "villas", with a plot in front—the inevitable plot with which so many of us Scotsmen have to console ourselves for glens and mountains lost. There were spotless white curtains on the windows.

I struck gently on the knocker of the door, and so fully and foolishly had I got the idea into my noddle that he would be glad to see me—why, heaven knows!—that when the great man himself opened the door I involuntarily took a step forward as if to enter.

But the door was only half opened. Davidson blocked the passage, and, with an arm stretched out to the wall, he let me see, without a word being spoken, that I was as far as I should get, and a little further than he wanted.

I knew him at once from his portraits. He looks exactly as he appears in them. He was quite well-groomed and shaven, and looked as if he ate well and slept o' nights. What struck me most was the clear white of his eyes. He has large and quickly moving eyes that make me think of some abnormal bird's, and as he swung them about—anywhere but in my direction—the white of them almost mesmerized me. I felt myself listening in a half-dwalm.

"What do you want?" he shot at me, as if I were a cadger. "My name is ——," I stammered. "I come from Greenock, and I have been asked by the Greenock Burns Club——" But I got no further.

"Ah! I never go to Burns Clubs," he interjected hurriedly. "I never go anywhere. I never see anyone. I am not like other men. People ought to think of these things."

I tried to stammer out that I was sorry to have troubled him, and that I did not think—— "There it is, you did not think!" he broke in.

[1] William Wallace.

"You *should* have thought. You should have said" (this with finger tapping forehead and eyes fixed on some far horizon), "here is a man different from other men! I must not treat him like other men! I must think, think, think! I must not go knocking at his door and expect to be received. I must write to ask if he will receive me."

There was just one more shot in my locker—the message to him from Dr Wallace about the "Random Itinerary" articles, and I delivered it by this time reduced to so mean and abject a frame of mind I would have let a blind cripple kick me.

"What made him ask *you* to call?" he exclaimed passionately. "He has written to me already. Doesn't he understand I'm very busy? Perhaps in three months I may send him something."

All this time he hardly once glanced at me, but darted his eyes here and there over my head, and ever kept his arms across the entrance. When he had finished the above confession of faith—in himself, he let his eyes drop on me for a second, shoved out a perfunctory hand to shake mine, and then slammed the door shut.

I crawled down the path like the veriest worm. When I got round the corner, however, I began to get something like myself back, and I cursed along the whole terrace. Then I simply roared with laughter. It was all so funny! Yet the man looked as sane as any man could be, his eye was alive with expression; his mouth was firm, his whole aspect capable.

Of course, I don't suggest that his keeping me standing at his door showed a mental squint—probably *you* will say it showed the highest wisdom, almost amounting to second sight. But, really, isn't he a queer chap? Is it pose or is it an unhappy temperament?'

The work with which Davidson was then preoccupied was his trilogy, *God and Mammon*, a huge dramatic blank verse poem of ideas. Alexander Scott has observed that Davidson 'could not altogether escape from the less pleasant aspects of the Scottish Victorianism in which he had been brought up' and that his poems in praise of a godless universe are as remarkable for their narrow fervour and their denunciation of different points of view as the polemics of Knox three and a half centuries earlier.

In the first part of the trilogy, *The Triumph of Mammon*, the old Christian world is pulled down about our ears. The heir to the throne of Thule renounces God just before taking the sacrament of marriage. He overthrows the attempts of his brother and his father, King Christian, to win him back to his old beliefs, and in defence of his right to disbelieve, and, incidentally, his manhood, is forced to kill both of them, thus touching off the classical mechanism of tragedy. He then assumes the throne of Thule, and the first part of the trilogy ends with Mammon declaring his high purpose to the rejoicing multitude.

In the second part, *Mammon and His Message*, Mammon tries to bring about the new state of his dreams. With an army behind him, he sets out on a course not dissimilar to those taken by the major dictators of the 'twenties and 'thirties of the present century. The old, the ugly and the poor are to be put down as an affront to the ideal state. Harlots are to reform and lawfully bear children, or suffer horrible punishment. Such threats carry Mammon so far. But he must convince those whose minds he cannot threaten, proving that his ruthless means justify his prophetic ends. This he finds less easy. Anselm, the Papal legate at Thule, who is a symbol of the old Christian order, argues with him that God allows wrong to flourish on earth for his own good reasons. Mammon will have none of it. He declares God to be:

> The cowardice of men flung forth to fill
> With welcome shadow an imagined void—
> Which never was, which by no chance can be.
> The unconscious ether fills the universe,
> Omnipotent, omniscient, omnipresent. . . .
> Afraid of mystery men explained the unknown
> As something immaterial—spirit, God.
> But there's no mystery hidden in the unknown,
> There's nothing in the unknown; there's no unknown.

In vain does Anselm protest. Mammon tries to force Anselm to change his creed:

> Say after me, 'Get thee behind me, God;
> I follow Mammon.' Say it! Say it!

Anselm refuses, so Mammon kills him. Mammon's principal supporter, one of those well-meaning men who get caught up idealistically in the wake of Hitlers, Mussolinis and Mammons, only to find themselves entangled anew in cruelty and horror, is shocked at the nature of the old man's death. His protest includes the significant line, 'the pace of life exceeds our staying power'.

Unfortunately, the last part of this strangely powerful and prophetic allegory, which would perhaps have more clearly revealed the poet's visionary purpose, was never written.[1] The pace of life exceeded Davidson's own staying power.

Sir William Rothenstein, who drew a sketch of Davidson in 1895 for the fourth *Yellow Book*, has preserved a pathetic recollection of the ageing poet:

> For some reason I coupled Davidson with William Watson, perhaps because I often met them together at the Hogarth Club when Lane was entertaining his authors, and I wanted to draw them together. Davidson was willing, but William Watson preferred to sit alone. Looking at my drawing of Davidson, Max[2] remarked on the subtle way in which I had managed his toupee: greatly to my surprise, for I had not noticed, to Max's amusement, that he wore one. How much more observant was Max than I! He told me that Davidson was far from wishing to look younger than in fact he was, but having to depend on journalism for a living, he feared a bald head would prejudice his chances.

The critic C. L. Hind wrote of Davidson's last days:

> His fine brain was disturbed by megalomania; he brooded darkly, incensed because the world would not take him at his own valuation. We met often at the old Hogarth Club. One conversation I remember well—on suicide. I thought that he was discussing it as an intellectual exercise. Lionel Johnson, a wraith of a man, the gentlest of souls, hovered around us that evening smiling his enigmatic smile, amused at our vehemence.

One of those who still believed in Davidson's potential ability was George Bernard Shaw. In 1908 Shaw made a generous gesture. Various second-hand accounts of what happened between Shaw and Davidson have been published. Not long before his own death, Shaw sent me a first-hand account of the sad business.

> I urged Davidson to cast aside all commercial considerations and write the great poem I believed he had in him expressing to the full

[1] According to Priscilla Thouless it was 'to show not only that Mammon could transcend every evil he could do, but also every evil that could be done to him'.
[2] Max Beerbohm.

his Lucretian Materialism. He replied that there was nothing he desired more, but that he could not afford it, as all his time was taken up writing potboilers to support himself and his dependants. I asked him how much he had to earn, and how long it would take him to write the poem. He said £500 a year, and six months. I sent him £250 and told him to go ahead with the poem, and give me half the profits until I was paid. The result was disastrous. Davidson was so overwhelmed by this endowment that he resolved to give me a great surprise and make an immense sum of money for me by writing, not the Lucretian poem, but a popular historical melodrama. He forgot that if he could not do this for himself, he could not do it for me. The melodrama was quite useless commercially: no manager would touch it. He had thrown away his big chance; and instead of asking me for another £250, which I would have given him, he drowned himself. Meaning to do him a service I had killed him. Meaning to inflate my bank balance he had knocked £250 off it. It was a tragi-comedy and a great pity.

There were other factors which led Davidson to commit suicide—or, as he would have put it, to rejoin unconscious matter —which he regarded as a man's unchallengeable privilege. On his last day of life, he wrote the preface to his final book of poems and posted the manuscript to his publisher. What Grant Richards, for whom Davidson had for some years been reading manuscripts, found when he opened the parcel in his London office next morning was this:

The time has come to make an end. There are several motives. I find my pension is not enough; I have therefore still to turn aside and attempt things for which people will pay. My health also counts. Asthma and other annoyances I have tolerated for years; but I cannot put up with cancer. . . .

Davidson's body was by then floating in the English Channel.

Up in Scotland, Christopher Murray Grieve (Hugh McDiarmid) read of Davidson's death, and later recorded the impact it made on him in a fine poem in which he saw Davidson's 'small black shape by the edge of the sea' as 'God through the wrong end of a telescope'.

Grieve once described Davidson as 'the only Scottish poet to whom I owe anything at all, or to whom I would be pleased to admit my debt'. Grieve's assessment of Davidson now, fifty years later, is included in this volume. While Davidson's influence on Eliot was largely a technical one, his influence on Grieve was much more general. It is impossible for a student of Davidson's work not to be struck by the many similarities between the approaches of both Davidson and Grieve to poetry and to the poet's rôle as prophet. Both delight in rhetoric. Both strive consciously after all-embracing universality, for greatness in the biggest sense. Both necessarily fail in their epic strivings for similar reasons. But Grieve, of course, has produced many more perfect poems than Davidson, who—in spite of the nobility and force of his later poems—could rarely subject his wide-ranging ideas to the intellectual discipline necessary to channel the perfect poem.

Nevertheless, the greatest British playwright of his day admired Davidson's work. The greatest Anglo-American poet and the greatest Scots poet of our day both endorse the playwright's admiration. For this poet of ideas who lived before his time has still much to say to us. He was an outsider. Yet courage was his to the end: and courage does not age.

> My feet are heavy now, but on I go,
> My head erect beneath the tragic years.
> The way is steep, but I would have it so;
> And dusty, but I lay the dust with tears,
> Though none can see me weep; alone I climb
> The rugged path that leads me out of time. . . .

2

A POEM must stand or fall by the force of its own integrity, and whether the poet wrote it under the influence of whisky or opium, or under the bed concealing himself from the broker's men, is of no account. A good poem creates its own permanent influence, which remains active even if the poem is laid aside or lost for several centuries. It is the intuitive knowledge of this fact that enables poets to face up to every kind of neglect and insult which society or circumstance may heap upon them, and still go on developing the special kind of creative energy that is theirs alone.

When considering the work of a poet as prolific and as un-self-critical as Davidson, especially in view of the special circumstances brought about by the nature of his Will, it may be worth the reader's while to become acquainted with the poet's own views on his art.

In *Sentences and Paragraphs*, a collection of sayings of an epigrammatic nature which Davidson published in 1893, there are a number of observations on the nature and uses of poetry, which call for no comment.

The want of poetical power is the impelling force in the case of most versifiers. They would fain be poets, and imagine that the best way is to try to write poetry, and to publish what they write. They will never see their mistake. *Equus asinus* still believes that the possession of an organ of noise is sufficient, with a little practice, to enable him to sing like a nightingale.

Like all bad habits, the indulgence is unrestrained, imaginative composition soon tyrannizes over the writer, be he small or great. In youth incontinence of utterance is expected, and has marked the earliest work of some of the greatest men of letters; but it is an unnatural fury that drives septuagenarians into the market-place with indiscretions and ineptitudes, with thoughts that should be secret and feelings that should be shamefaced.

Except to the poet, the age of poetry is always past.

If one has a healthy mind it is wholesome to go from extreme to extreme, just as a hardy Russian plunges out of a boiling bath into the snow.

The chief hindrances in the consideration of any matter are the thoughts of others. It is not so much a test of genius to think originally as to know what one actually does think. Some men upon most subjects have two judgments: a public one for daily use, and a private one which they deceive themselves into the belief they never held.

There are decent, honest men who opine the opinions of others, persuaded that they are their own; few indeed can detach their proper thought from the mass of ideas.

A certain barrister of some note, who makes about a thousand a year by his novels and stories in addition to his professional earnings, is said to have filled up his income-tax schedule as follows: Profession, Law—so much; Trade, Literature—so much. True or not, we are here face to face with one fact which has been recognized ever since the opening of Grub Street, and with another not perhaps so generally known. That literature, or rather writing, for nearly two hundred years now, has been followed as a trade by hosts of needy or prosperous scholars and others, all the world knows. Does it know also that those who take cheerfully to writing as a trade, and nothing else, are often the very men who, from their circumstances, might be expected to produce literature? The ever-increasing numbers, ambitious of literary distinction, who flock to London yearly, to become hacks and journalists, regard the work by which they gain a livelihood as a mere industry, a stepping-stone to higher things—alas! a stepping-stone on which the great majority of them have to maintain a precarious footing all their lives. But they do not choose the inferior work that pays: they offer, or think they offer, the public, through the publishers, bread; but the public—still the thought of the hack—wants stones, and these they are forced sorrowfully to supply. What wonder if they sometimes take to laying about them with scorpions! And what wonder if they often accept their fate and become fat and flourishing!

It may be said broadly that there are three kinds of poets—employing the word as inclusive of all verse-writers: those who turn out garments, those who put some kind of body into the stuff they shape, and those who inform their work with a soul. As a rule it will be found that diction and passion, the garment and the body, are most delicately wrought, and, in the old-time phrase, most loftily built, when the essence of the poetry is spiritual, when it has a soul. Few poets consciously endeavour to make only garments; but it is the misfortune of many that they are unable to carry their creative labours further. There is no necessity, in the nature of things, why those poets who, doing their best, succeed in making only the trappings of poetry, should be anathematized, except, perhaps, when the trappings are badly made—and that is what too often happens if there be no measurement to work to, no body to fit. Even then, however, it is wise and humane not to invoke the thunder. Torture always undid its purpose; let the critic be merciful.'

26

A Rosary (1903) contains some of Davidson's 'middle period' observations on literature, including definitions of style and stylism.

Style is always imperceptible: stylism one notes at once. Stylism is the attempt to achieve style—that is to say, the attempt of self-consciousness to be unconscious; the attempt to say something not in its own manner, but in a predetermined manner. Scott has style; Stevenson is a stylist.

His admiration for men of action is reflected when he writes:

The power of the pen has been grossly exaggerated. Napoleon, not Goethe, made the modern world. Everybody knows the life of Napoleon and its meaning, 'the tools to him that can handle them'.

Perhaps with his own vast ambitions in mind he declared:

People who cry for the moon should never be blamed. It is necessary always and at all times to cry for the moon. There is a proverb in Scotland, 'If ye bode (ask) for a silk goon ye'll get the sleeve o't,' and if we persistently cry for the moon we may be rewarded in time with a piece of green cheese.

Like most poets who, for any reason, outrun their popularity, Davidson did not believe that literary criticism had any value.

Literary criticism implies a contradiction in terms. It is impossible to give an account of one art except by another. Browning, the boys' poet *par excellence*, couldn't have written the 'criticism as well as the poetry', in spite of his threat. Wagner gave a more or less successful account of his endeavour and meaning in music by the medium of another art, Literature namely . . . Rosetti was able to employ two arts as the complements of each other in a very special way. But literary criticism is impossible. Literature already exists in literary form.

This is hardly a tenable proposition, though characteristic of the writer who announced: 'A poet is always a man of inordinate ambition and of inordinate vanity.'

The views of a poet who so markedly divided his attention between rhymed verse and blank verse on the qualities of the two media are of special interest. Davidson dealt with this matter in the first part of an essay 'On Poetry', which was printed at the back of *Holiday and Other Poems* (1906):

Rhyme is probably seven hundred years old; still, I suppose it may be called modern. The fall of Constantinople, the invention of printing, and the Renascence make a great frontier between the new and the antique; but, behind this frontier and buttressing it, there stretches back, among other spurs and ranges, the quasi-popularization of poetry by the Minnesingers and the Troubadours in the gorgeous decadence of the last crusades. These liberal minstrels led Poetry out of the study and the scriptorium into the court and the camp, and arrayed her for her novel rôle in the new-fangled frippery of rhyme. The nun became a glee-maiden, or rather, as they could not lead about a naked goddess, they paraded instead a bedizened harlotry, very delightful and much more convenable than the austere and unadorned beauty of rhymeless verse; and since the days of the Minnesingers, the Jongleurs, Trouvères, and Troubadours, and from Dante to Mr Swinburne, the exquisite adornment of rhyme has corrupted the ear of the world. Rhyme is a property of decadence; but decadence in any art is always the manure and root of a higher manifestation of that art. Dante and Petrarch quickly subdued the new wanton mode. In time there came into being the French Alexandrine and the English rhymed pentameter, and, as the crown of the whole poetical aim of the world, English blank verse. Yet, at its best, rhyme is a decadent mode, although great ages and great poets have made it the vehicle of crescive work. It is a special flattery of the external ear; it is as rouge on the cheek and belladonna on the eye; or it is an excrescence like a sixth finger, 'a wasteful and ridiculous excess'. I am not thinking of bad poetry, but of the best. Take the first quatrain of Shakespeare's seventy-third sonnet:

> That time of year thou may'st in me behold
> When yellow leaves, or none, or few, do hang
> Upon those boughs which shake against the cold,
> Bare ruin'd choirs, where late the sweet birds sang.

The rhymes of this quatrain toll like a dead-bell; we pass from a sombre forest to a dim cathedral; the fancy is overwhelmed with vision, both detailed and indefinite, in order to bring the rhymes about; there is a feeling of effort, as of a thing achieved; and it is the rhyme that achieves. It is not the poet, not the poetry, but the rhyme that requires this laborious 'or none, or few'; it is the rhyme that requires those superbly imagined 'boughs which shake against the cold' to shift at once as by the waft of a rococo conjurer's wand into 'bare ruin'd choirs'. Yet it is beautiful, it is poignant; it entertains the fancy, fills the eye and ear, and touches the soul.

But, now, let Macbeth say the same thing without rhyme:

> My way of life
> Is fallen into the sere, the yellow leaf.

No comment is necessary; the hair of the flesh stands up, and one feels that there is a great gulf fixed between rhyme and blank verse.

I know nothing so entertaining, so absorbing, so full of contentment, as the making of blank verse; it is a supreme relief of nervous tension, the fullest discharge of emotion, the greatest deliverance of energy; it satisfies the blood and the brain, the bones and the marrow. Whether the reader be friend or foe, I wish him to regard my authority in the matter; and I bring as a credential a passage of my own blank verse. The passage I quote is not my own selection, nor would I have chosen it; it has been singled out by others.

> Undo the past!
> The rainbow reaches Asgard now no more;
> Olympus stands untenanted; the dead
> Have their serene abode in earth itself,
> Our womb, our nurture, and our sepulchre.
> Expel the sweet imaginings, profound
> Humanities and golden legends, forms
> Heroic, beauties, tripping shades embalmed
> Through hallowed ages in the fragrant hearts
> And generous blood of men; the climbing thoughts
> Whose roots ethereal grope among the stars
> Whose passion-flowers perfume eternity,
> Weed out and tear, scatter and tread them down;
> Dismantle and dilapidate high heaven.

That the above passage should be both fluent and powerful stands to reason, as it is the long-matured, spontaneous expression of a permanent mood of the world which has its crises in reformations and revolutions, and which in the twentieth century will arm itself for action more heated and more terrible than all the wars and persecutions of the past, and which will restore to religion, art, and letters a youth and a freshness more radiant and more fragrant than they ever wore even in their prime and pristine vigour. The world is only beginning. We have done nothing, said nothing, sung nothing. The history of the past is the history of one empire at a time. Now several empires must compete together. The world will yet know more essential personalities than Buddha and Christ, greater men than Caesar and Napoleon, deeper passion and wider humanity than Shakespeare's, a music still more elemental than Wagner's, a sadder soul than Schopenhauer's, a more triumphant intellect than Nietzsche's, beauty more enthralling than Helen's. Even the man in the train knows that we live in the newest times; it is borne in upon him, half fearfully, half ecstatically, as he reads his morning newspaper, that the world is barely adolescent, and that its majority cannot be until after a thousand years of war between the East and the West, when the yellow man and the white man have fought it out on equal terms, and learnt which is master.

Poetry is Matter become vocal, a blind force without judgment. Much there is a poet can control; he acquires a vocabulary, sifts and sorts; he can select the theme of his poem, and the weight and convolutions of his brain determine the power and variety of his rhythm, but the purport of his poetry is not within his own control. A hard saying, in England of all places; but I mean it. Milton undertakes to justify the ways of God to man in *Paradise Lost*. He may have done so in terms of his theology—who cares? That is not the poetry of his epic; the poetry of it is the love of Adam and Eve, and the rebellion of Satan. He who set out to justify the ways of God to man lives in the heart and soul of every stockbroker, soldier, adventurer, artist, poet, by one line which no one who knows it ever forgets: 'Better to reign in Hell than serve in Heaven.'

After elaborating on Shakespeare's use of blank verse, Davidson goes on:

But in spite of the superiority of blank verse, the exquisite adornment of rhyme will continue to corrupt the ear, the seeing ear as well as the hearing ear; it is mainly with the ear the reader of poetry sees. A speculative writer suggested once that the eye is a degenerate organ, the malversation of some higher perceptive power, inconceivable in range and penetration. By such an analogy the ear was originally intended for vision as well as audition; the tympanum and tympanic membrane, when one considers them, are clearly a combination of mirror and sounding-board. Why the mirror remains inoperative we cannot say, since no blind beggar has, up to this time of writing, developed vision by light refracted through the auditory canal; but the reader of poetry knows very well that the optic nerve responds like a taut string to the rhymes that vibrate in the membranous labyrinth

30

of the ear; and he knows also that the prompt vision flashed on the inward eye by the percussion of rhyme has injured the palate of this double sense of seeing and hearing, so that the subtler sound and loftier sight transmitted by the rhythm of blank verse are hardly possible now to his over-stimulated, frayed, and angry senses. Poetry is therefore as little understood as it ever was, rhyme—as necessary to the general verse-reader as brandy to the brandy-drinker—being only an ornament. A sense of shame, indeed, struggles vainly towards a blush in the cheeks of the many-headed when it turns its galaxy of eyes on a page of blank verse; its subconscious feeling is of something indecorous, if not indecent. The feeling is just. Blank verse is nude poetry, barbarous and beautiful, or athletic and refined, but always naked and unashamed.

Like many a nineteenth-century artist, Davidson theorized more vociferously the older he grew. Both parts of *God and Mammon* carry Epilogues. In the Epilogue to *The Triumph of Mammon* (1907), Davidson sets forth his views on the Christian background to English poetry. It is odd to find Greenock-born Davidson referring to Burns as being possessed of 'a great English imagination', but it is clear from the context that what he really means is 'British' and equally clear from his exposition of Burns's views on marriage that he has not read his Burns very carefully.

The liberation of the mind and imagination of England upon the severance with Rome found its most fitting expression and illustration in the plays of Shakespeare; and the poetry of that religion which had filled the fancy with the mystic sacrifice of the Host and the adoration of the Virgin is finally eliminated in the pedantic God of the decadent *Paradise Lost*. Between the times of Shakespeare and Milton and the times of Burns and Wordsworth there is no great English poetry. When Dryden's imagination seeks for a home in the Universe it beats the air in strong low-pitched flight from a classical apotheosis of Cromwell through the doctrine of the restored Anglicanism of Charles II to the doctrine of the hot-house Catholicism of the much-maligned James; and the rapid wing of Pope upon the same errand can attain no higher heaven than the 'Rosicrucian doctrine of spirits'. Not until Burns does a great English imagination live again in a conception of the Universe. It is the old conception: the world suspended by a hair from the floor of Heaven above a flaming Hell. And it is also the old morality in almost every respect, and especially concerning women, because a great poet is always a great lover: Burns, like Shakespeare, was much troubled with love: the passionate union of men and women seemed to him sinful without the sanction of marriage.

Wordsworth's relation to Burns is parallel with Milton's relation to Shakespeare. Milton and Wordsworth wrote with affection, admiration, and a certain patronage of Shakespeare and Burns; the austerity of both—Milton in his youth, Wordsworth in his maturity—was tempered by the wide humanity of their greater predecessors; but religion which is emotional in Shakespeare and Burns becomes doctrinal in Milton and Wordsworth. Nevertheless, Wordsworth's popular reputation as the most original of English poets is not groundless: he sought a way out of Christendom, and hoped to find an abiding-place for his imagination in the mind of man. In the mind of man, however, there was nothing to be found but the old spiritual world and the old morality. Wordsworth accepted the defeat, and prophesied a day when the mind of man should contain, not a symbol of the Universe, but the Universe itself, feeling a presence that disturbed him with the joy of elevated thoughts.

> a sense sublime
> Of something far more deeply interfused,
> Whose dwelling is the light of setting suns,
> And the round ocean and the living air,
> And the blue sky and in the mind of man:
> A motion and a spirit that impels
> All thinking things, all objects of all thought,
> And rolls through all things.

A very perfect and prophetic account, under the old spiritual guise, of the omnipresent ether, the material source, substance and inspiration of all things. If I could make men know the meaning of that!—the greatness and the beauty and the entire sanctity of a purely material world!'

The need for that upheaval in the arts which manifested itself early in the twentieth century, and most conspicuously in England after the First World War, was also foreseen by Davidson:

There is no change in the substance of English poetry from Chaucer's time to mine: it subsists hitherto in two worlds, a material world and a spiritual world, the latter allowing and disallowing the

32

former; Chaucer remains as modern as Burns, Tennyson as antique as Spenser, and the plays of Shakespeare hold the stage. It is as impossible to say how great Shakespeare was as it is unnecessary to rake a sordid story out of the sonnets. The autobiographies of all artists will be found in their works, in their pictures, their plays and poems, sonatas and operas. The men whose lives I wish to know thoroughly are warriors, kings, statesmen, financiers, explorers, because their work is their conduct; it is their behaviour in the world that counts; whereas with the artist it is what he transmutes his life into that counts. Villon was a *souteneur* and a thief: he translated one of the most luckless lives into the most beautiful and enduring poetry. If Shakespeare, as some would make out, was a pandar and a pederast, so much the greater artist he to have grown all that strength and beauty with such misfortune gnawing at the roots. For me he is great enough without these ascriptions and almost as happy as Homer in the oblivion that has swallowed up his life. A poet's work is born with his life, certain; but time puts away the life as a midwife disposes of a caul: we forget the inchoate wrappage, and remember only the art; and Shakespeare is so great that his art would have sunk deep into the eternal memory of the world even had he been as unhappy as his worst detractors could desire. To have had to write *Macbeth* would have killed such men as Tennyson and Browning; but after *Macbeth* Shakespeare passed through the agony of *Lear*, the naive and awful passion of *Othello*, the bitter dead-sea brine of *Timon*, the intellectual wantonness and world tumult of *Antony and Cleopatra*, and the lust and shambles of *Troilus and Cressida*. He passed through that and came out of it sane, sweet, tender and majestical in the enchanted isle of *The Tempest*; therefore Shakespeare is loved of all man. Shakespeare delivered himself up without reserve or afterthought to the dual world of his time, and to the undiscovered worlds of wonder upon the earth itself: we forget sometimes that the world was not always known; nor can the most detachable imagination ever again realize what it meant to live upon an earth two-thirds of which were still unexplored. Shakespeare's mind and imagination lived more intensely than any other man's in Heaven and Hell, and in the mythical realm of gods and fairies; and his passion beat against the iron bars of religion and morality never dreaming of a way out of Christendom. In the great plays I have mentioned, and in *Hamlet* and the others, man is shown once for all comporting himself in Christendom; and as the English stage still lives and moves and has its being in the Christian economy, fable and morality, there is no occasion to write great plays for it: it is impossible to supersede Shakespeare in his own world. Shakespeare is the limit in the literature of the past; we must have a new world in order that the utmost may once more achieve itself in literature.

33

In the Epilogue to *Mammon and His Message* (1908) Davidson expressed his disbelief in a political panacea for the ills of the world:

It is not a revolution I propose: revolution is nothing. We have had revolution again and again: it is chronic in Europe—a readjustment of rich and poor, an uneasy turning over of a part of Christendom without actual change. Were Socialism a realized ideal to-morrow there would be no actual change: only the dead corpse of Christendom floating up again upon the tide. Socialism, like Christianity, proceeds upon the assumption that men are not what they are. There is little difference between Feudalism and Socialism. Socialism would lay hands upon the earth and its products, upon man and his labour, not heroically, in arms, by superior craft and intellect, as Feudalism did, but unheroically, by means of representative government (which is no government), by universal suffrage, bargains with the mob, and the prate of parliamentarians. Socialism is the decadence of Feudalism; that is to say, it is less than nothing. At its very utmost it is only a bad smell; rejoicing in itself very much at present, as bad smells are wont to do.

What was needed, Davidson felt, was an increase in the development of Man's powers of imagination:

It is by the imagination that men live; imagination, the poles of which are vanity and malice, is the joy of life. The senses are the ducts of the feelings; imagination is the gulf and the retort that swallows and transmutes sight and sound, touch and taste, and all emotion, passion, thought, into beauty and delight, into power and achievement. Imagination must be fed, it must be supported. If it be starved, both the individual and society degenerate and pass down into the lowest class.

Davidson elaborated his views on the uses of imagination with a vivid piece of reportage about a Cornish Fair, which is worth quoting in its entirety:

It is by imagination that religion or any cause lives and prospers. If you doubt this of the Salvation Army, attend its meetings. You can do so with me, now, at the Land's End. It is the annual carnival in West Penwith. The town stands on a slope, and the Fair Ground is behind on the top of the hill. At the entrance to the Fair the Salvation

Army occupies a stance every night, like a lion in the path; but nobody is scared, and with two exceptions, none pay any heed. You and I visit the Fair thrice at night, and on each occasion pause to listen to the music and speech of the Salvationists. The Captain is a remarkably handsome man, very conscious of his good looks; these, his curly black hair and a concertina being his armour. His voice in singing is not very effective, and we never hear him speak. He seems to you and me not insincere, but shallow and good-tempered, having no depth of nature or strength of character with which to be either sincere or insincere. They are singing 'Dare to be a Daniel' on our first visit. Present: the Captain, the band, half-a-dozen women and a few girls. The townsfolk and people of the countryside by the hundred troop past, going and coming: but except ourselves no one regards the Salvationists: they are not seen, not heard, not thought of, not even consciously ignored. We think this remarkable. No county in England was more responsive to Wesley than Cornwall. Perhaps the fanfare and glaring symbolism of the Salvation Army are against it in districts where the more intellectual, more ascetic method of Wesley prevailed. We grant that, wishing to make every allowance, but we remember the Fair. When the hymn is finished the Captain smiles and nods to a woman who steps forward and speaks. She wears the bonnet, jacket and skirt of the Army; is short and small; her face, lean and grey; her eyes, large, sunken, hard and hot. She gives her testimony eloquently; convicted and convinced; there is no question of her entire sincerity. She had been a great sinner, without hope or help; she had ceased to care for anything; her one desire had been to die, to forget and be forgotten. But Christ came her way, lifted her burden and took her hand; and she grasped His with both hers, and she'll never leave go. 'No,' she cries, with her hot, hungry eyes, devouring the evening sky, 'I'll never leave go.' 'Amen!' sobs the drummer—a six-foot-three drummer— thin, angular, tremendously in earnest. The woman raises her voice to reach the passers-by. She says that she has been saved from Hell and an eternity of torment, and why should they, poor deluded sinners going to the Fair, not be saved also? She speaks for less than five minutes, beginning as if let off by a trigger, and finishing as if pulled up by a powerful brake. The Captain starts a hymn on the instant, the band joins in, the women and children sing mechanically, 'I do believe, I will believe', the whole having the effect of some extraordinary automatic engine. The Salvation Army is, indeed, a not unsuccessful attempt to make people religious by machinery.

On our second visit there is a smaller muster of the Army. After the hymn, again a woman speaks. She also begins as if she had been let off; goes at a breathless pace, but articulately and eloquently; and finishes like the shutting up of a telescope or the snapping of a trap.

She is trim and neat, young, pretty and as innocent as the daisies, but convicted and convinced. She speaks with profound sorrow of her sins; but 'praised be God, the burden has been lifted. I was never a bad woman, but that was all the worse for me, as I couldn't feel my sin. At last I knew I had been a sinner from my birth, rejecting Christ and His Salvation. I felt that I was hanging over the pit; I felt the flames; I was singed in the fire. But Christ plucked me like a brand from the burning three weeks ago today. Still the memory of my sins and of my former lost state comes over me sometimes, and I hear behind me the flames hissing and I smell the smoke. But I am saved from Hell fire and sure of Heaven through the blood of Christ.' Then she appeals to the passers-by: 'The Fair is certainly the gate of Hell; you are going straight to damnation. Will you not turn into the narrow way and be saved?'

On the third night the muster is still scantier. The bland, smiling Captain, with cheeks like steaks, smooth white brow, and curling black hair, touches his concertina in a dilettant style and starts the hymn: the band blares out the tune, 'Dare to be a Daniel' once more, and the few girls present sing shrilly. The drummer is the spokesman, a very halting orator: one secret of the success of the Salvation Army is the scope it gives women, who are, generally, more eloquent than men. The drummer blurts out short, incomplete sentences, but leaves no doubt that he also has been convicted and convinced; that for him Christ is a living person; Hell a terrible material fact; and Heaven a glorious certainty.

What we note every night is this: Although there could be no question of the sincerity of the three speakers; although they had evidently been convicted of sin and were now convinced of salvation they were, there, at the gate of the Fair, utterly unconvincing. They themselves seemed to realize it: the appeal to the unconverted became perfunctory and a formality in such unseasonable circumstances; and they were content to build each other up in the faith. The reward of the speakers was the applause of their comrades; the 'Amens!' and 'Glory, Hallelujahs!' that greeted the reiterated doctrine of blood and fire. Now as an evangelist, as a messenger, as a gatherer from the highways and byways, we find the Fair much more convincing than the Salvation Army; and we visit it, with clear consciences, every night.

It is an extensive Fair. The further from London the bigger the Fair. When there is no music-hall within a hundred miles of the town all the showmen in England may cut and come again. On the clouded sky at night the ruddy oil-lamps of the stalls and the pale electric lights of the merry-go-rounds and the theatres spread a mixed lacquer of tarnished gold, dusky emerald, and swarthy purple visible from all parts of the town and for miles round, alluring the fancy of the young and the old, a convincing sign in the heavens of entertainment, frolic and festivity. The drum of the Salvation Army and the shrill voice of renunciation are no match for that wanton light in the sky. We enjoy the Fair on each visit, examining it with unabated curiosity. It is much more interesting than the Salvation Army. In the very gate, just beyond the blood-red flag, two nauseous youths are trying to sell a pornographic print, a feeble affair, commonly sold in the streets of London at night. They have no market that we can see. Near them a stout couple exhibit a 'happy family', rats, cats, monkeys, dogs, weasels, guinea-pigs, all in one cage. Sweetstuff stalls line the way, and broad-faced, brazen-lunged, huge-fisted men do a roaring trade in a leprous-looking compound that cuts like cheese and is sold in chunks at two-pence. Eight merry-go-rounds occupy one side of the main street of the Fair, with cocoa-nut shies and other adventurous traffic between. Opposite the merry-go-rounds are the boxers, the fat women, the tethered footballs, the strength-tests, etc. Two of the merry-go-rounds are small, old-fashioned, and hand-driven; the others are gigantic wheels, cirques of gondolas, of motor cars, of centaurs, ostriches, boats, dazzling with electric light, and grinding out against each other from mechanical organs *Tannhäuser* and 'Stop yer ticklin', Jock', grand opera and nigger melodies. At the top of the High Street of the Fair a helter-skelter in the form of a lighthouse trundles uproarious troops in a spiral journey from the sky to the earth; and, further up the hill with a wide space in front for the admiring crowd, two gorgeous theatres are filled and emptied six times a night at twopence, threepence, and sixpence. The penny gaff is a thing of the past even at the Land's End in Fair time. A bioscopic exhibition is the staple of entertainment in these theatres. There is no play in either of them; a little dancing, feats of strength, ventriloquism, and comic songs punctuate the various series of pictures. Mingling with the discord of the music, the pipe, whistle and scream of the roundabouts, the cries of the cheapjacks and stall-holders, and the laughter, shouts and shrieks of the crowd, the whirr of the electric generators, the pulse of the whole, sounds fitfully as we pass and repass the hot shaking engines in travail with their dynamos.

For three days and three nights this travelling suburb of frivolity is thronged by Cornish crowds from all the towns, villages and farms in the neighbourhood. All classes are represented, all ages, with one mood, with one will in all—the intention to be happy. Of one thing all the frequenters of the Fair are certain, on each visit at least, that happiness is possible here below; and they are all bent on one more bid for it, seeing that their carnival has come round again.

What they really enjoy is a satisfied imagination. The bioscope and the merry-go-rounds, the flaring and dazzling lights, the tumult of music, and the uproar of the crowd overbrim the imagination of the frequenter of the Fair. He has only to walk up the hill to be filled with light and colour, sound and movement, to have his imagination clothed as with a Universe of suns and systems. He enjoys because his imagination is replenished: there is no other enjoyment. At the gate of the Fair stands religion, preferring to the ephemeral vanities of the travelling showman a vision of the Universe itself; but the vision is not patent, and the Fair is; and so the pleasure-seeker passes in. To the Salvationist at the gate the Fair is without interest or attraction; he sees something much more dazzling, and infinitely greater; which has also the fascination of terror: he sees a vision of the Universe. Imagination requires nothing less than the infinite. If the religion or cause is to be enduring and of world-wide acceptance, imagination must clothe itself in the Universe: not in a theory, which is vision dead and mummified, but in a palpable, tangible, grossly material Universe such as the Salvation Army provides—a world which was created by the spoken word of a personal God; a temptation and fall; an incarnation, atonement and resurrection; an awful fiery Hell of everlasting pain, and a glorious Heaven of perpetual enjoyment. The peace and joy they experience is the test and the proof of their religion to the converts of the Salvation Army. What they really enjoy is also enjoyed by the visitor to the Fair, a satisfied imagination.

Finally, a statement of the aims which constituted Davidson's poetic creed a few months before he took his own life:

A dead historian wrote a book upon the rise of Rationalism; an interesting book of its kind, containing references to many facts. But there cannot be a rise of Rationalism. There was only a decay of Imagination. The instinct of the holothure, a sea-cucumber of the Philippine Islands, amounts to genius. This admirable living alembic devours coral sand in its native haunts, and grows plump and shapely on the sapless fare. Shift him to some zone of the sea where his sandy pastures are not, and immediately he ejects the whole of his digestive canal, and all the organs connected with it. Rationalism of the right kind; but not a 'rise' of Rationalism. If the holothure, having rid himself of what had become unnecessary and ineffective, remained satisfied with the change, he would soon cease to be a holothure; but no sooner has this consummate genius sloughed out his declassed viscera than he evolves an apparatus entirely in harmony with his new habitat.

The so-called Rise of Rationalism was an ejectment of the Imagination. The form and substance of Imagination had been in all ages a symbol of the Universe that tended always to a more remote symbolism, to intensified supernaturalism, to a grosser superstition, the more definitely men took it for the Universe itself. Rationalism evacuated the old form and substance of Imagination, and rested there wondering what had happened. One thing had happened: the world had come to an end for the Rationalists. By Imagination men live.

Surgery has found out that, unlike the holothure, man can get along without a stomach; but Art knows very well that the world comes to an end when it is purged of Imagination. Rationalism was only a stage in the process. For the old conception of a created Universe, with a fall of man, an atonement, and a Heaven and Hell, the form and substance of the Imagination of Christendom, Rationalism had no substitute. Science was not ready; but how can poetry wait? Science is synonymous with patience; poetry is impatience incarnate. If you take away the symbol of the Universe in which since the Christian era began, poetry and all great art lived and had their being, I, for one, decline to continue the eviscerated Life-in-Death of Rationalism. I devour, digest, and assimilate the Universe; make for myself in my Testaments and Tragedies a new form and substance of Imagination; and by poetic power certify the semi-certitudes of science.

3

THE editor who finds himself called upon to present a selection from another man's work has a duty to set down the principles by which he has made his choice. I have included in their entirety all Davidson's poems which seem to me more or less without any major blemish. Many of his poems are represented here by extracts simply because in each case the extract seemed to me to make more of an impact cut away from the weedy tangle in which it was set, and which often completely obscured it. But a more detailed account of the manner in which I exercised my editorial responsibilities may help the reader to approach the poems themselves with a better sense of their relevance to the poet's total output than if the poems were simply presented without comment.

Both the examples from *Fleet Street Eclogues*, as might be expected in a young poet, show Davidson much concerned with 'those who sang of love'. 'St Valentine's Eve' is also interesting in that it reflects the bitterness of his Scottish sectarian upbringing, and because of Percy's concluding recommendation. Davidson's Scottish richness of descriptive nature-writing is in the mainstream of a tradition which may be traced unbroken—Scotland having had no indigenous Augustan interlude—from the *Moral Fables* of Henryson to the work of the Lallans Makars and the Anglo-Scots poets of the present century.

Ballads and Songs is in many ways Davidson's best book of verse. His splendid picture of Greenock taken from 'A Ballad in Blank Verse of the Making of a Poet' is highly characteristic, in spite of its Shakespearian echo ('This old grey town, this firth, this farther strand spangled with hamlets'). This volume also contains two of Davidson's other anthology pieces, 'Thirty Bob a Week', and 'In Romney Marsh'. The method of generating generalized sympathy for the under-dog—which Davidson uses in 'Thirty Bob a Week'—a method which (though still sometimes resorted to by Trade Unionists in the middle of the Welfare State Twentieth Century) has now become decidedly old fashioned—is also reflected, though less tersely, in 'London' and in 'A Loafer'. Scottish literature is curiously deficient in town poetry. In these poems and others like them, Davidson gives us the 'feel' of the sights and sounds of late-Victorian London, an aspect of poetry largely ignored by most of the major poets of the period.

The companion piece to 'In Romney Marsh', 'A Cinque Port', is weakened by a poor concluding line, and illustrates what romanticists might call the erratic nature of Davidson's inspiration, but what I prefer to call, though sympathetically, his frequent disinclination to get down to the sheer hard labour of poem-making, the anvil work. One reason for the lack of revision and polish, for his too-ready acceptance of stale padding to fill out the good things which came to him spontaneously, may have been the economic pressure from which he was never able to win completely free. Incredible as it may seem to modern readers, many Victorian poets depended for a livelihood almost solely on the money they made out of their poetry, augmented by the writing of those detailed reviews of other men's books for which newspapers then had space and readers had leisure to study. Davidson was probably the last of the nineteenth-century poets who tried to make poetry their principal support. The result was that in his total output there are perhaps a dozen poems perfect of their kind, and fifty or sixty poems which, though flawed by haste or carelessness, contain a sufficient number of good things to make them still worth reading. The 'Spring' and 'Summer' extracts are taken from four poems of the seasons, and illustrate the method I have used to salvage such good things.

In *New Ballads* the most ambitious piece is undoubtedly 'A Woman and Her Son'. Davidson's religious doubtings were at first basically of the kind that troubled Arthur Hugh Clough, and to some extent Matthew Arnold. But Davidson, brought up in a Scottish evangelical household, felt intense bitterness whenever he remembered his upbringing, soured by:

> . . . our evangelist, whose little purse
> Opened to all save us; who squandered smiles
> On wily proselytes, and gloomed at home.

No one who has not experienced at first hand the oppressive narrowness and arrogant stupidity of the extreme sects in the Scottish Church can have any real idea how Davidson must have suffered from his father's religious castigations. 'A Woman and Her Son', though it is by no means free of mawkish sentimentality, describes the poet's breakaway from the emotional tyranny of his parents ('bigots—fateful souls that plague the gentle world'), and is the first poetic evidence of Davidson's personal solution—an existentialist one.

> . . . There's no heaven.
> Your children are resolved to dust and dew;
> But, mother, I am God: I shall create
> The heaven of your desires. . . .

The other extracts which I have included from *New Ballads* are, with one exception, merely slight and pleasant. The exception is 'A Northern Suburb', a sympathetic piece of period social criticism. In his later work, Davidson broke new poetic ground in two directions. He was among the first to make poetry out of the everyday speech of ordinary people: and, abandoning Christianity as an exhausted creed, he took up a standpoint which we may now recognize as existentialist and experimented with the poetry of science. His scientific poetry belongs to the last ten years of his life when, according to his first posthumous editor, R. D. MacLeod, Davidson's 'mind was in decline'. MacLeod felt unable to countenance the passionate anti-Christian outlook which animated much of the poet's later work, and the literary reputation of his subject suffered in consequence. The *Testaments* show a break with the style of the earlier lyric verse. Though there are fine passages in the remaining lyrical volumes, Davidson's style showed little further development in this direction.

'War Song', from *The Last Ballad*, is a singularly outspoken attack on the ethics of war, its armies, 'huge brutes in dumb distress'. The bitterly cynical anti-military mood may have been inspired by A. E. Housman's *A Shropshire Lad*, which was by then well set upon its course of fame. 'Holiday at Hampton Court' and 'In the Isle of Dogs' once again reflect Davidson's feeling for the common man's London.

From the second series of *Fleet Street Eclogues*—Davidson was never at his best when he tried to refurbish in modern dress classical eclogue or folk ballad—I have chosen only one small atmospheric excerpt.

The Testament of a Man Forbid (1901) is, in many ways, the best of Davidson's Testaments, and I have included it in its entirety. Psychiatrists could no doubt read into it evidence of the early stages of the mental disorder from the taint of which Davidson's family was not free. The unscientific reader will simply accept it as the *cri de cœur* of an Outsider who, however much he protests that he likes being 'outside', protests too much. *Holiday and Other Poems* (1906) provides a lyric interlude in Davidson's final period. 'A Runnable Stag', which has become an anthology piece, captures the excitement of the chase yet allies the reader's sympathies with the hounded beast. The only other sizable piece which I have taken from this collection is Davidson's admirable rhetorical salute to Nelson.

From *A Rosary*, a volume of prose and verse fragments put together in 1903, presumably for what little it might bring in quickly, I have taken 'The Wastrel'. Long after the Greenock days were far behind him, memories of the nagging evangelism with which he associated the place apparently still troubled him. 'The Wastrel' is plainly a period piece, but the minister it describes has his counterpart today in the pulpit of many a church in the Highlands of Scotland.

I have not included anything from *The Testament of a Vivisector* —which curiously anticipates D. H. Lawrence's[1] 'thinking with the blood' idea—not because the notions it expresses must seem rather absurd to modern minds, but because it is extremely difficult to find an extractable passage which can stand by itself. From *The Testament of a Prime Minister* I have taken Davidson's vision of judgment; a judgment in which the meek followers of Christ, 'apostles, martyrs, votarists, virgins, saints', are charged with having thrown away the gift of life and are condemned to eternal fire, having proved to be:

> Deniers, slanderers, fools that turned to scorn
> The perfect world I made superb in strength
> Unparagoned in beauty.

Those who inherited Davidson's heaven were:

> The kings, the conquerors, the wise, the bold.
> The rich, the proud, and all the lusty lives
> That took their power and pleasure in the world.

In our own 'Age of Defeat', when the weak and the ineffectual have been made the heroes and heroines of our fiction, Davidson's views may seem repugnant. Yet they should not be too readily condemned. He was quite certain that life was meant to be lived to the full.

[1] As Thouless put it: 'In the imaginative work of both is embodied a vision of life in which sexual love is the centre of existence. But whereas Lawrence confines us in a beautiful but suffocating tunnel, Davidson bursts open the walls of the round world of our childhood so that we can lean out and see the stars beyond, the "matter" of his praising.'

Sometimes, however, he seems to be shouting to keep up his own courage. Even to many of his contemporaries, this roaring boy attitude seemed forced. Yeats has recorded Davidson's compliment to himself as having 'blood and guts', qualities which the Scots poet (quite properly) found lacking in most of the other associates of the Rhymers' Club. And Vincent O'Sullivan, who liked Davidson rather more than did Yeats, said that Davidson 'did his best to play the steak-and-ale, none-of-your-nonsense Britisher of the type created by Henley. But it was easy to see that he was other than that. . . .' Sir George Douglas also knew Davidson in this mood. He remembered Davidson 'extolling the glorious rough-and-tumble of the poet's life, its unexpected ups and downs, the rough and smooth of it. He delivered the tirade in Piccadilly, standing on the pavement. And who would ever have suspected that 'twas all bravado—that his mouth was full of bitterness and his heart nigh breaking at the moment?'

Most of Davidson's verse plays are lengthy exercises in that dreary post-Shakespearian blank verse which has trapped so many minor poets into extended dullness. But Davidson's major work, the uncompleted trilogy *God and Mammon*, bursts through the plodding limitations of linguistic pastiche. Only two sections of the work were written before Davidson took his own life, and it is therefore impossible to be sure what ultimate fate Davidson had in store for his hero Mammon, the man of action who, by the authority of force, sought to destroy the values of the western world's Christian civilization and replace them with the calculated values of science and reason. It is impossible for later generations, with the experience of practical dictatorships still freshly in mind, to overlook the prophetic nature of many of Prince Mammon's utterances. I have included long extracts from *The Triumph of Mammon* and from *Mammon and his Message* for several reasons. In the first place, Davidson's Mammon symbolizes a recurring human phenomenon. (It remains to be seen whether the masses, with whom the ultimate power now lies in our modern democracies, can exert the energy and self-discipline to permit the democratic order to function efficiently enough to make the reappearance of a new Mammon unnecessary.) In the second place, Davidson's rhetoric is here experienced at its most powerful. The passion which inspired it, under different circumstances, might have enabled him to become a successful major poet, instead of a major *poet manqué* whose technique and self-discipline could not regulate the flow from its eruptions. There is a third reason, too, why *God and Mammon* should be well represented in any competent selection of Davidson's work. The poet himself set considerable store by these verse plays. No assessment of his achievement which does not take *God and Mammon* into account can be a balanced one.

From his posthumous book *Fleet Street and other Poems* (1909) I have taken some shorter atmospheric pieces; 'Snow', a remarkable poem for its time, and two longer poems 'The Crystal Palace' and 'The Testament of Sir Simon Simplex Concerning Automobilism'. In his last months, Davidson finally lost interest in the *tutti-frutti* Tennysonian afflatus, and turned his attention to the kind of social comment in verse which has subsequently found favour with many twentieth-century English poets.

The selection ends, by a slight violation of chronology, with the poet's epitaph upon himself, taken from *The Testament of John Davidson*.

The condition in Davidson's Will which made it impossible for any new selection of his work to be published during the period of copyright has acted disadvantageously upon his reputation. His first editions—in most cases there never were any others—have been eagerly sought after by a small band of Davidson enthusiasts, some of whom have publicly exaggerated his poetic stature. In the absence of a reprinted volume of selected poems the general reader has been unable to test these claims by objective standards. A false expectancy was thus built up; an expectancy dispersed when the first selection to appear after the expiry of the copyright period, *Poems and Ballads* edited by R. D. MacLeod, merely reprinted Davidson's own *Selected Poems* of 1903, adding a few other poems from the earlier volumes. By this selection, Davidson was made to appear as an inferior conventional minor Victorian with inexplicable flashes of near-genius. The forward-looking aspect of his gifts and the influence he exerted over writers as diverse as T. S. Eliot and Hugh McDiarmid was completely overlooked. The main purpose of this more extensive selection is to reinstate Davidson's reputation by remedying those defects.

A complete edition of Davidson's poems is probably out of the question in these days of high costs. Possibly it is not even desirable. But undoubtedly a biographical study of the poet will eventually be produced, in spite of his wish that nothing of the sort should be written, for we exceed our rights when we seek to dictate to posterity. It seems more than probable that Davidson's biography will be the work of an American scholar, since modern economic conditions have resulted in almost all recent important studies of Scots authors being produced on the other side of the Atlantic. Furthermore, the bulk of Davidson's surviving letters are preserved in America.[1]

In my own view, extravagant claims should not be made for Davidson's achievement *vis-à-vis* that of his contemporaries. The hardship and bigotries of his upbringing, the troubles of his family and his almost constant struggle with poverty, all operated against him. His circumstances never allowed him the time to be a perfectionist. His temperament prevented him from fully developing his abilities. Consequently, much of his poetry comes to us with the mud of technical deficiency on its boots. But at least that mud still reeks of the life and times through which he strode and strove.

'He resented the unknown and loathed all forms of weakness,' wrote Holbrook Jackson in *The Eighteen Nineties*. 'He could not accept life as he found it, and his philosophy reflects his objection to circumstance and fate, actuality and condition, in a passionate claim for control over destiny and power, and over life itself.'

Jackson was writing of Davidson almost fifty years ago.

He remains a fascinating character and a poet the force of whose personality commands at least as much attention as his actual literary achievement.

---

[1] There is a large Davidson collection at Princeton University. See 'The Quest for John Davidson', by J. B. Townsend: *Princeton University Chronicle;* Vol. 13, 1952.

JOHN DAVIDSON

Influences and Influence

HUGH McDIARMID

MR MAURICE LINDSAY and others have commented on the fact that I have been greatly influenced by John Davidson in my poetic development. That is true and I have gladly admitted it, and in this connection said in a broadcast talk on the occasion of Davidson's centenary that Davidson is 'the only Scottish poet to whom I owe anything at all, or to whom I would be pleased to admit any debt'. He is certainly the one who interests me most between the great Makars of the fifteenth and sixteenth centuries and one or two of my own contemporaries, save for Fergusson and Burns, some Gaelic poets like Alasdair MacMhaighstir Alasdair, and Duncan Ban MacIntyre, and two Latin ones, George Buchanan and Arthur Johnstone. With these exceptions, there is scarcely any Scottish poet in these three or four centuries of any technical or intellectual interest whatever. Davidson stood out head and shoulders above all the Scottish poets of his own time. He alone had anything to say that is, or should be, of interest to any adult mind.

I did not know him personally, but I remember as if it were yesterday how the news of his suicide by walking into the sea off Penzance in March 1909, when I was a lad of seventeen, affected me. I felt as if the bottom had fallen out of my world.

Later I wrote of this:

I remember one death in my boyhood
That, next to my father's, and darker, endures;
Not Queen Victoria's but, Davidson, yours,
And something in me has always stood
Since then looking down the sandslope
On your small black shape by the edge of the sea
A bullet-hole through a great scene's beauty,
God through the wrong end of a telescope.

Young as I was, it had already become obvious that I was destined to be a poet, and my parents were alarmed at the thought that I was about to devote my life to so unprofitable a business—a business in which there was no money and no security. They, and other friends, were already representing to me that versifying should be kept, if at all, merely as a spare-time affair. In Davidson's death, coming on top of such anxieties as to the course my life was to take, I probably had a premonition of what Muriel Stuart, a subsequent Scottish poet friend of mine, wrote in this connection:

Thou knowest at what cost
Thy sleep was taken on those awful hills—
What thou hast gained, and lost;
Thou knowest, too, if what thou art fulfils
The pledge of what thou wast,
And if all compensates the poet's wreath
That wounds the brow beneath.

Why did Davidson influence me so greatly? There were a number of reasons. I have always been a minority man. Andrew Lang, reviewing Davidson's Fleet Street Eclogues, said: 'Sometimes, after a "torrent of applause" you hear one lonely belated pair of hands clapping. Such a demonstration is this of mine.' But in several cases, Davidson's, Charles Doughty's, Francis Adams's, I have been one of the 'few but fit' whose isolated hand-clapping has preceded, and still precedes, any torrent of applause.

Readers of my Scottish Eccentrics and other books will know that I have shown that in so far from being 'kindly brither Scots', 'canny' or anything of that sort, the majority of distinguished

Scots have always conformed to the character the world long before ascribed to the Scot in the epithets '*fier comme un Ecossais*' and '*piper in naso*', and also to the even earlier conclusions that the Scots were men of curious and restless learning, versatile, with little or no use for 'water-tight compartments', and likely to be found bestraddling several disciplines at once. Davidson was of this type. As Israel Zangwill said of him:

Fancy and imagination, wit and humour, fun and epigram, characterization and creation and observation, insight and philosophy, passion and emotion and sincerity—all are his. Nothing is lacking from that long catalogue by which Imlac convinced Rasselas that it was impossible to be a poet . . . and all these glorious gifts have found vent in the most diverse artistic or inartistic shapes—novels, dramas, eclogues, ballads, Reisebilder—some written for the market, but the bulk in defiance of it . . . and it is significant that all Mr Davidson's chief successes are won when he surrenders himself to the inspiration of the modern. This is the work we need. Let all who wish to see how the poet's eye may body forth, not the shapes of things unknown, but what is much more taxing, the shapes of things known and disesteemed, betake themselves in haste to *Fleet Street Eclogues*, *In a Music-Hall*, *A Random Itinerary*, and the rest of Mr Davidson's books.

Mr James Douglas emphasized another element in Davidson which, even in 1909, had begun to prompt my own mind in the direction in which it was most fully to find itself two or three decades later. 'He states fact in terms of poetry,' wrote Mr Douglas, 'and the statement scars one's consciousness. He is the first poet to digest the new wonders of science which have subtly changed the old cosmogony, and made the very foundations of existence crumble away.' It was this element which made me write my own second poem to Davidson—it is in Scots, but, Englished, it says:

The relation of John Davidson's thought to Nietzsche's is more important than all the drivel about 'Home, Sweet Home' four million cretins iterate. And if we can't throw off the world, let us hear of no 'Old Gray Mother' at all, but of Middle Torridonian Arkose with local breccias, or the pillow lavas at Loch Awe.

49

Another Scot, the poet-scientist Ronald Campbell Macfie, also wrote poems on Davidson, but he was—as also was Alfred Noyes, another poet who handled scientific subject-matter—far less modern, far less truly scientific in his thinking, than was Davidson.

Davidson was a true prophet:

The insane past is the incubus: the world is really a virgin world awaking from a bad dream. These are some of the seeds of the new thing I bring, of the new poetry which the world will make. Poetry is the flower of what all men are maturing in thought and fancy; I reap a harvest unsown; I come a hundred years before the time—that time foreseen by Wordsworth—'when what is now called science, familiarized to men, shall be ready to put on a form of flesh and blood.'

Albeit it is perhaps more difficult than ever just at this moment to indulge the stupendous and typically Scottish humour that could hazard 'the poetical suggestion' that it is the presence of the incommunicable elements—dead gases, ghosts of elements herding with the vapour of dissolution nitrogen—

that maintains the mechanical mixture of the oxygen and the nitrogen of the air: were their ghostly frontier eliminated, the two main members of the atmosphere would unite chemically, forming protoxide of nitrogen, which is laughing gas. Great Pan! How close we are to that rare old fantasy, that the crack of doom will be a universal shout of laughter!

What Davidson, alone of Scottish poets, did was to enlarge the subject matter of poetry, assimilate and utilize a great deal of new scientific and other contemporary material, pioneer in poetic drama and other forms, and recognize thus early the exhaustion of English, writing as he did:

> Our language is too worn, too much abused,
> Jaded and overspurred, wind-broken, lame—
> The hackneyed roadster every bagman mounts,

and, above all, to write urban poetry (a development Scots like

Alexander Smith and Thomas Hood had heralded, but which subsequent Scots poets failed to carry on, although already the rural Scotland of the bulk of Scottish poetry had been succeeded by the depopulation and dereliction of vast areas and the crowding into a narrow industrial belt of over two-thirds of our population.) Yet most of our versifiers continued to write nostalgic, pseudo-pastoral rubbish about an Arcadian life which had no relation to the facts at all. For the matter of that, they are still doing so.

The most powerful influences on Davidson himself were Ibsen and Nietzsche—both first translated into English by Scots —Nietzsche by Thomas Common and Ibsen by William Archer. Davidson was very well read in English literature, and also in French and German literatures, but like most modern Scots seems to have known little or nothing about Scottish literature nor suspected for a moment that he was posing himself against a hopelessly wrong background in English literature. When Dr Gertrud von Petzold in her *John Davidson und sein geistiges Werden unter dem Einfluss Nietzsches* (Leipzig 1928), referring to one of Davidson's stories, expresses regret that he did not give us 'more Jenny Macintoshes and fewer Earl Lavenders, more Scottish heart-notes of so full and deep a resonance, and fewer super-clever London extravaganzes', she was expressing what most discerning critics have felt about practically all modern Scottish writers (e.g. Lady Cynthia Asquith's remarks on Sir J. M. Barrie, as 'defeated by the English', and her regret that he did not stay in Scotland and become the great Scottish dramatist he might have been), but the pity was that, like most educated Scots of the time (and still) he was never put at school in possession of more than a few discrete fragments of his proper national heritage, and, above all, that he was unable to realize the far greater suitability of Scots for the expression of his ideas than English could ever afford. Social protest, espousal of the cause of the underdog, anti-religion, materialism, Rabelaisan wit, invective—all these find a place much more easily and prominently in the Scottish than in the English tradition. All these are salient features of Davidson's work. In short, like Byron, he was a Scottish, not an English, poet, although he used an alien language, and had apparently no knowledge of the independent Scottish tradition. Nor did he express much in the way of Scottish nationalist sentiment. However, as Professor B. Evans says, 'the sympathy is with the Scots throughout'.

In other directions, however, Davidson's work was a valuable corrective to two of the greatest curses that have affected, and still affect, modern Scottish literature—namely, the superfluity of minor versifiers and absence of poetic ambition, and, associated with that, the horrible humility of mediocrity which is willing enough, as Kierkegaard said, to admit any one to its ranks on an equal footing, but prompt to crucify any one who dares to lift his head above the ruck.

Statements of Davidson's with regard to these last two matters have stuck in my mind, and influenced me profoundly, for over forty years. For example, from *A Rosary*:

> A poet is always a man of inordinate ambition and of inordinate vanity. In his heart he says, 'I want my poetry to be remembered when Homer and Dante and Shakespeare are forgotten.'

Again, specially applicable to the Scottish scene, from *Sentences and Paragraphs*:

> The want of poetical power is the impelling force in the case of most versifiers. They would fain be poets, and imagine that the best way is to try to write poetry and to publish what they write. They will never see their mistake. *Equus asinus* still believes that the possession of an organ of noise is sufficient, with a little practice, to enable him to sing like a nightingale.

In another paragraph in the same book, Davidson hopes of those who were reconstructing Provencal poetry, that 'the head, as of yore, and not the heart, will be the source of the poetical passion' —a view I share, and have frequently propounded, in a far wider context. I have always agreed with him, too, that 'if one has a healthy mind it is wholesome to go from extreme to extreme, just as a hardy Russian plunges out of a boiling bath into the snow'.

But the most important element in Davidson—and one to which attention should be directed most strongly if justice is to be done to him at last and his influence brought to bear effectively where it is most needed—is expressed in the following passage from *A Rosary*. It re-echoes for today what has been a main theme of Scottish poetry back through Burns to Henryson and Sir David Lyndesay:

Poetry is not always an army on parade: sometimes it is an army coming back from the wars, epaulettes and pipeclay all gone, shoeless, ragged, wounded, starved, but with victory on its brows; for Poetry has been democratized. Nothing could prevent that. The songs are of the highways and the byways. The city slums and the deserted villages are haunted by sorrowful figures, men of power and endurance, feeding their melancholy not with heroic fable, the beauty of the moon, and the studious cloisters, but with the actual sight of the misery in which so many millions live. To this mood the vaunted sweetness and light of the ineffective apostle of culture are, like a faded rose in a charnel-house, a flash of moonshine on the Dead Sea. It is not now to the light that 'the passionate heart of the poet' will turn. The poet is in the street, the hospital. He intends the world to know it is out of joint. He will not let it alone. Democracy is here; and we have to go through with it. The newspaper is one of the most potent forces in moulding the character of contemporary poetry. Burns's eyes were open; Blake's, perhaps, for a time; and Wordsworth had profound insight into the true character of man and the world; but all the rest saw men as trees walking; Tennyson and Browning are Shakespearian. The prismatic cloud that Shakespeare hung out between poets and the world! It was the newspapers that brought about what may be called an order of pre-Shakespearianism. It was in the newspapers that Thomas Hood found the 'Song of the Shirt'—in its place the most important English poem of the nineteenth century; the 'woman in unwomanly rags plying her needle and thread' is the type of the world's misery. The 'Song of the Shirt' is the most terrible poem in the English language. Only a high heart and strong brain broken on the wheel of life, but master of its own pain and anguish, able to jest in the jaws of death, could have sung this song, of which every single stanza wrings the heart. Poetry passed by on the other side. It could not endure the woman in unwomanly rags. It hid its head like the fabled ostrich in some sand-bed of Arthurian legend, or took shelter in the paradoxical optimism of 'The Ring and the Book'. It is true William Morris stood by her when the priest and the Levite passed by.

He stood by her side, he helped her; but he hardly saw her, nor could he show her as she is. 'Mother and Son', his greatest poem, and a very great poem, is a vision not of a woman, but of a deserted Titaness in London streets; there was a veil between him also and the world, although in another sense, with his elemental Sigurds, he is the truest of all pre-Shakespearians. But the woman in unwomanly rags, and all the insanity and iniquity of which she is the type, will now be sung. Poetry will concern itself with her and hers for some time to come. Not much of the harlot: she is at ease in Zion compared with actual woe. The offal of the world is being said in statistics, in prose fiction; it is besides going to be sung. There it is in the streets, the hospitals, the poor-houses, the prisons; it is a flood that surges about our feet, it rises breast-high, and it will be sung in all keys and voices. Poetry has other functions, other aims; but this also has become its province.

As J. Russell Lowell said, 'Not failure, but low aim is crime.' Davidson almost alone of the poets of his time cannot be convicted of this crime. This is his great significance. It is time that was fully realized.

from

Fleet Street Eclogues

[1893]

St Valentine's Eve

MENZIES PERCY

PERCY

A-moping always, journalist? For shame!
Though this be Lent no journalist need mope:
 The blazing Candlemas was foul and wet;
 We shall be happy yet:
Sweethearts and crocuses together ope.

MENZIES

Assail, console me not in jest or trope:
Give me your golden silence; or if speech
 Must wake a ripple on the stagnant gloom
 Of this lamp-darkened room,
Speak blasphemy, and let the mandrake screech.

PERCY

Dread words—'tis Ercles' vein—and fit to teach
The mandrake's self new ecstasies of woe,
 Have passed my lips in blame of God and man.
 Now surely nothing can
Constrain my soul serene to riot so.

57

But you are old; the tide of life is low;
No wind can raise a tempest in a cup:
   Easy it is for withered nerves and veins,
   Parched hearts and barren brains
To be serene and give life's question up.

PERCY

Although no longer chamber-doors I dup
For willing maids (that never conquered me);
   Though unimpassioned be my tranquil mind,
   And all my force declined,
My quenchless soul confronts its destiny—
But tell me now what ghastly misery

Peeps from the shadowy cupboard of your eye?
   This chastened mouth in white and gold is dressed,
   Lilies and snowdrops blessed:
Be shriven by me as you were now to die;
Shrove-tide is come.

MENZIES

                        Confessions purify.
My skeletons I will uncupboard straight;
   And if you think me pitiful and weak,
   I pray you do not speak,
But go and leave me lonely with my fate.—
My daily toil has irked me much of late:

Of books that never will be read I write
   What, save the anxious authors, no one reads,
   And chronicle the deeds

Of Fashion, Crime, and Council, day and night.
Once in a quarter when my heart is light.

I write a poem in a weekly sheet,
  To lie in clubs on tables crowned with baize,
  Immortal for seven days:
This is the life my echoing years repeat.

PERCY

The very round my aged steps still beat!

MENZIES

And brooding thus on my ephemeral flowers
  That smoulder in the wilderness, I thought,
  By envy sore distraught,
Of amaranths that burn in lordly bowers,
Of men divinely blessed with leisured hours.

And all the savage in my blood was roused.
  I cursed the father who begot me poor,
  The patient womb that bore
Me, last of ten, ill-fed, ill-clad, ill-housed;
I cursed the barren common where I browsed

And sickened on the arid mental fare
  The state has sown broad-cast; I cursed the strain
  Whence sprang my blood and brain
Frugal and dry; I cursed myself the heir
Of dreadful things that met me everywhere:

Of uncouth nauseous vennels, smoky skies;
  A chill and watery clime; a thrifty race,
  Using all means of grace
To save their souls and purses; lingering lies,
Remnants of creeds and tags of party cries—

Scarecrows and rattles; then I cursed this flesh,
   Which must be daily served with meat and drink,
   Which will not let me think,
But holds me prisoner in the sexual mesh;
I cursed all being, and began afresh—

My education and my geniture,
   Which keep me running always from the goal,
   Or stranded on Time's shoal—
In naked speech, a sixpenny reviewer,
A hungry parasite of literature.

PERCY

No reasoning can meet so fierce a mood.
   I'll tell you of a journalist instead,
   These many winters dead,
Who out of evil could distil the good.
He found his lot untameable and rude,

And sometimes ate what beggars had disdained
   Left at the donor's door. Once on a time
   A wanton youthful rhyme
I read him with my tears and heart's blood stained,
Wherein of Fate I bitterly complained.

He praised my rhymes; then said, 'The Poet's name
   Is overhallowed; and the Statesman's praise
   Unearned; unearned the bays
That crown the Warrior; Beauty, Art, I blame,
For Love alone deserves the meed of fame.'

MENZIES

I understand you not.

Be still and mark.
'And so,' he said, 'though I am faint and old,
   High in my garret cold—
While on the pane Death's knuckles rattle stark,
And hungry pangs keep sleep off—in the dark,

'I think how brides and bridegrooms, many a pair,
   With human sanction, or all unavouched,
      Together softly couched,
Wonder and throb in rapture; how the care
Of ways and means, the thought of whitening hair,

'Of trenchant wrinkles fade when night has set,
   And many a long-wed man and woman find
      The deepest peace of mind,
Sweet and mysterious to each other yet.
I think that I am still in Nature's debt,

'Scorned, disappointed, starving, bankrupt, old,
   Because I loved a lady in my youth,
      And was beloved in sooth.
I think that all the horrors ever told
Of tonsured men and women sable-stoled,

'Of long-drawn tortures wrought with subtle zest,
   Of war and massacre and martyrdom,
      Of slaves in Pagan Rome—
In Christian England, who begin to test
The purpose of their state, to strike for rest

'And time to feel alive in: all the blight
   Of pain, age, madness, ravished innocence,
      Despair and impotence,
The lofty anguish that affronts the light,
And seems to fill the past with utter night,

'Is but Love's needful shadow: though the poles,
    The spangled zodiac, and the stars that beat
    In heaven's high Watling Street
Their myriad rounds; though every orb that rolls
Lighting or lit, were filled with tortured souls,

'If one man and one woman, heart and brain
    Entranced above all fear, above all doubt,
    Might wring their essence out,
The groaning of a universe in pain
Were as an undersong in Love's refrain.

'Then in a vision holy Time I see
    As one sweet bridal night, Earth softly spread
    One fragrant bridal bed,
And all my unrest leaves me utterly:
I sometimes feel almost that God may be.'

MENZIES

You touch me not. I, stretched upon the rack
    Of consciousness, still curse. Women and love?
    I would be throned above
Humanity. Yet were I God, alack!
I think that I should want my manhood back,
Hating and loving limits—

PERCY

                    Ah! I know
How ill you are. You shall tomorrow do
    What I now order you.
At early dawn through London you must go
Until you come where long black hedgerows grow,

With pink buds pearled, with here and there a tree,
    And gates and stiles; and watch good country folk;
    And scent the spicy smoke
Of withered weeds that burn where gardens be;
And in a ditch perhaps a primrose see.

The rooks shall stalk the plough, larks mount the skies,
    Blackbirds and speckled thrushes sing aloud,
    Hid in the warm white cloud
Mantling the thorn, and far away shall rise
The milky low of cows and farmyard cries.

From windy heavens the climbing sun shall shine,
    And February greet you like a maid
    In russet-cloak arrayed;
And you shall take her for your mistress fine,
And pluck a crocus for her valentine.

MENZIES

In russet-cloak arrayed with homespun smock
And apple cheeks.

PERCY

I pray you do not mock.

MENZIES

I mock not, I shall see earth and be glad:
London's a darksome cell where men go mad.

'THOSE WHO SANG OF LOVE'

(*from* St Swithin's Day)

. . . Three things are worthiest knowing,
And when I know them nothing else I know.
I know unboundedly, what needs no showing,
That women are most beautiful; and then
I know I love them; and I know again
Herein alone true Science lies, for, lo!
Old Rome's a ruin; Cæsar is a name;
The Church?—alas! a lifeboat, warped and sunk;
God, a disputed title: but the fame
Of those who sang of love, fresher than spring,
Blossoms for ever with the tree of life,
Whose boughs are generations; and its trunk
Love; and its flowers, lovers.

from

Ballads and Songs

[1894]

'GREENOCK'

(from A Ballad in Blank Verse of the Making of a Poet*)*

His father's house looked out across a firth
Broad-bosomed like a mere, beside a town
Far in the North, where Time could take his ease,
And Change hold holiday; where Old and New
Weltered upon the border of the world.

'Oh now', he thought—a youth whose sultry eyes,
Bold brow and wanton mouth were not all lust,
But haunted from within and from without
By memories, visions, hopes, divine desires—

'Now may my life beat out upon this shore
A prouder music than the winds and waves
Can compass in their haughtiest moods. I need
No world more spacious than the region here:
The foam-embroidered firth, a purple path
For argosies that still on pinions speed,
Or fiery-hearted cleave with iron limbs
And bows precipitous the pliant sea;
The sloping shores that fringe the velvet tides
With heavy bullion and with golden lace
Of restless pebble woven and fine spun sand;
The villages that sleep the winter through,
And, wakening with the spring, keep festival
All summer and all autumn: this grey town
That pipes the morning up before the lark
With shrieking steam, and from a hundred stalks

Lacquers the sooty sky; where hammers clang
On iron hulls, and cranes in harbours creak,
Rattle and swing, whole cargoes on their necks;
Where men sweat gold that others hoard or spend,
And lurk like vermin in their narrow streets:
This old grey town, this firth, the further strand
Spangled with hamlets, and the wooded steeps,
Whose rocky tops behind each other press,
Fantastically carved like antique helms
High-hung in heaven's cloudy armoury,
Is world enough for me. Here daily dawn
Burns through the smoky east; with fire-shod feet
The sun treads heaven, and steps from hill to hill
Downward before the night that still pursues
His crimson wake; here winter plies his craft,
Soldering the years with ice; here spring appears,
Caught in a leafless brake, her garland torn,
Breathless with wonder, and the tears half-dried
Upon her rosy cheek; here summer comes
And wastes his passion like a prodigal
Right royally; and here her golden gains
Free-handed as a harlot autumn spends;
And here are men to know, women to love.'

LONDON

Athwart the sky a lowly sigh
  From west to east the sweet wind carried;
The sun stood still on Primrose Hill;
  His light in all the city tarried:
The clouds on viewless columns bloomed
Like smouldering lilies unconsumed.

Oh sweetheart, see! how shadowy,
  Of some occult magician's rearing,
Or swung in space of heaven's grace
  Dissolving, dimly reappearing,
Afloat upon ethereal tides
St Paul's above the city rides!

A rumour broke through the thin smoke
  Enwreathing abbey, tower, and palace,
The parks, the squares, the thoroughfares,
  The million-peopled lanes and alleys,
An ever-muttering prisoned storm,
The heart of London beating warm.

from

A LOAFER

I hang about the streets all day,
  At night I hang about;
I sleep a little when I may,
  But rise betimes the morning's scout;
For through the year I always hear
  Afar, aloft, a ghostly shout.

My clothes are worn to threads and loops;
  My skin shows here and there;
About my face like seaweed droops
  My tangled beard, my tangled hair;
From cavernous and shaggy brows
  My stony eyes untroubled stare.

I move from eastern wretchedness
  Through Fleet Street and the Strand;
And as the pleasant people press
  I touch them softly with my hand,
Perhaps to know that still I go
  Alive about a living land.

For, far in front the clouds are riven;
  I hear the ghostly cry,
As if a still voice fell from heaven
  To where sea-whelmed the drowned folk lie
In sepulchres no tempest stirs
  And only eyeless things pass by.

In Piccadilly spirits pass:
  Oh, eyes and cheeks that glow!
Oh, strength and comeliness! Alas,
  The lustrous health is earth I know
From shrinking eyes that recognize
  No brother in my rags and woe.

I know no handicraft, no art,
  But I have conquered fate;
For I have chosen the better part,
  And neither hope, nor fear, nor hate.
With placid breath on pain and death,
  My certain alms, alone I wait.

THIRTY BOB A WEEK

I couldn't touch a stop and turn a screw,
    And set the blooming world a-work for me,
Like such as cut their teeth—I hope, like you—
    On the handle of a skeleton gold key;
I cut mine on a leek, which I eat it every week:
    I'm a clerk at thirty bob as you can see.

But I don't allow it's luck and all a toss;
    There's no such thing as being starred and crossed;
It's just the power of some to be a boss,
    And the bally power of others to be bossed:
I face the music, sir; you bet I ain't a cur;
    Strike me lucky if I don't believe I'm lost!

For like a mole I journey in the dark,
    A-travelling along the underground
From my Pillar'd Halls and broad Suburban Park,
    To come the daily dull official round;
And home again at night with my pipe all alight,
    A-scheming how to count ten bob a pound.

And it's often very cold and very wet,
    And my missis stitches towels for a hunks;
And the Pillar'd Halls is half of it to let—
    Three rooms about the size of travelling trunks.
And we cough, my wife and I, to dislocate a sigh,
    When the noisy little kids are in their bunks.

But you never hear her do a growl or whine,
    For she's made of flint and roses, very odd;
And I've got to cut my meaning rather fine,
    Or I'd blubber, for I'm made of greens and sod:
So p'r'aps we are in Hell for all that I can tell,
    And lost and damn'd and served up hot to God.

I ain't blaspheming, Mr. Silver-tongue;
  I'm saying things a bit beyond your art:
Of all the rummy starts you ever sprung,
  Thirty bob a week's the rummiest start!
With your science and your books and your the'ries about
                                                    spooks,
    Did you ever hear of looking in your heart?

I didn't mean your pocket, Mr., no:
  I mean that having children and a wife,
With thirty bob on which to come and go,
  Isn't dancing to the tabor and the fife:
When it doesn't make you drink, by Heaven! it makes you
                                                    think,
    And notice curious items about life.

I step into my heart and there I meet
  A god-almighty devil singing small,
Who would like to shout and whistle in the street,
  And squelch the passers flat against the wall;
If the whole world was a cake he had the power to take,
  He would take it, ask for more, and eat it all.

And I meet a sort of simpleton beside,
  The kind that life is always giving beans;
With thirty bob a week to keep a bride
  He fell in love and married in his teens:
At thirty bob he stuck; but he knows it isn't luck:
  He knows the seas are deeper than tureens.

And the god-almighty devil and the fool
  That meet me in the High Street on the strike,
When I walk about my heart a-gathering wool,
  Are my good and evil angels if you like.
And both of them together in every kind of weather
  Ride me like a double-seated bike.

That's rough a bit and needs its meaning curled.
　　But I have a high old hot un in my mind—
A most engrugious notion of the world,
　　That leaves your lightning 'rithmetic behind
I give it at a glance when I say 'There ain't no chance,
　　Nor nothing of the lucky-lottery kind.'

And it's this way that I make it out to be:
　　No fathers, mothers, countries, climates—none;
Not Adam was responsible for me,
　　Nor society, nor systems, nary one:
A little sleeping seed, I woke—I did, indeed—
　　A million years before the blooming sun.

I woke because I thought the time had come;
　　Beyond my will there was no other cause;
And everywhere I found myself at home,
　　Because I chose to be the thing I was;
And in whatever shape of mollusc or of ape
　　I always went according to the laws.

I was the love that chose my mother out;
　　I joined two lives and from the union burst;
My weakness and my strength without a doubt
　　Are mine alone for ever from the first:
It's just the very same with a difference in the name
　　As 'Thy will be done.' You say it if you durst!

They say it daily up and down the land
　　As easy as you take a drink, it's true;
But the difficultest go to understand,
　　And the difficultest job a man can do,
Is to come it brave and meek with thirty bob a week,
　　And feel that that's the proper thing for you.

It's a naked child against a hungry wolf;
    It's playing bowls upon a splitting wreck;
It's walking on a string across a gulf
    With millstones fore-and-aft about your neck;
But the thing is daily done by many and many a one;
    And we fall, face forward, fighting, on the deck.

IN ROMNEY MARSH

As I went down to Dymchurch Wall,
   I heard the South sing o'er the land;
I saw the yellow sunlight fall
   On knolls where Norman churches stand.

And ringing shrilly, taut and lithe,
   Within the wind a core of sound,
The wire from Romney town to Hythe
   Alone its airy journey wound.

A veil of purple vapour flowed
   And trailed its fringe along the Straits;
The upper air like sapphire glowed;
   And roses filled Heaven's central gates.

Masts in the offing wagged their tops;
   The swinging waves pealed on the shore;
The saffron beach, all diamond drops
   And beads of surge, prolonged the roar.

As I came up from Dymchurch Wall,
   I saw above the Downs' low crest
The crimson brands of sunset fall,
   Flicker and fade from out the west.

Night sank: like flakes of silver fire
   The stars in one great shower came down;
Shrill blew the wind; and shrill the wire
   Rang out from Hythe to Romney town.

The darkly shining salt sea drops
   Streamed as the waves clashed on the shore;
The beach, with all its organ stops
   Pealing again, prolonged the roar.

A CINQUE PORT

Below the down the stranded town,
　What may betide forlornly waits,
With memories of smoky skies,
　When Gallic navies crossed the straits;
When waves with fire and blood grew bright.
And cannon thundered through the night.

With swinging stride the rhythmic tide
　Bore to the harbour barque and sloop;
Across the bar the ship of war,
　In castled stern and lanterned poop,
Came up with conquests on her lee,
The stately mistress of the sea.

Where argosies have wooed the breeze,
　The simple sheep are feeding now;
And near and far across the bar
　The ploughman whistles at the plough;
Where once the long waves washed the shore,
Larks from their lowly lodgings soar.

Below the down the stranded town
　Hears far away the rollers beat;
About the wall the seabirds call;
　The salt wind murmurs through the street;
Forlorn the sea's forsaken bride,
Awaits the end that shall betide.

from SPRING

By lichened tree and mossy plinth
   Like living flame of purple fire,
Flooding the wood, the hyacinth
   Uprears its heavy-scented spire.

The redstart shakes its crimson plume,
   Singing alone till evening's fall
Beside the pied and homely bloom
   Of wallflower on the crumbling wall.

Now dandelions light the way,
   Expecting summer's near approach;
And, bearing lanterns night and day,
   The great marsh-marigolds keep watch.

SUMMER

I

The poets' May is dead and done
   That warm and soft came shoulder-high
On Leda's twins; for now the sun
   Scarce breaks the cold and cloudy sky.

But still by fields of grass and corn
   With mantling green like blushes spread,
The milk-maid in the early morn
   Trips with her milkpail on her head.

And still through mists that droop and float,
   Beside the river lingering white
Dew on his wings and in his note,
   The lark goes singing out of sight.

And still the hawthorn blossoms blow;
   The belted bee on nectar sups;
And still the dazzling daisies grow
   Beside the golden buttercups.

II

Glow-worm-like the daisies peer;
   Roses in the thickets fade
Grudging every petal dear;
   Swinging incense in the shade
The honeysuckle's chandelier
   Twinkles down a shadowy glade.

Now is Nature's restful mood:
  Death-still stands the sombre fir;
Hardly where the rushes brood
  Something crawling makes a stir;
Hardly in the underwood
  Russet pinions softly whirr.

III

  Above the shimmering square
    Swallows climb the air;
Like crystal trees the fountain's shower,
A-bloom with many a rainbow flower.

  Where the lake is deep
    Water-lilies sleep,
Dreaming dreams with open eyes
Enchanted by the dragon-flies—

  Azure dragon-flies,
    Slivered from the skies,
Chased and burnished, joints and rings,
Elfin magic wands on wings.

  Like an army dressed
    In diamond mail and crest,
The silent light o'er park and town
In burning phalanxes comes down;

  And lustrous ambuscades
    In glittering streets and glades,
Where daisies crowd or people throng,
Keep watch and ward the whole day long.

from

Fleet Street Eclogues

Second Series
[1895]

from MIDSUMMER DAY

I stand upon a lowly bridge,
    Moss-grown beside the old Essex home;
Over the distant purple ridge
    The clouds arise in sultry foam;

In many a cluster, wreath and chain
    A silvery vapour hangs on high,
And snowy scarfs of silken grain
    Bedeck the blue slopes of the sky;

The wandering water sighs and calls,
    And breaks into a chant that rings
Beneath the vaulted bridge, then falls
    And under heaven softly sings;

A light wind lingers here and there,
    And whispers in an unknown tongue
The passionate secrets of the air,
    That never may by man be sung:

Low, low, it whispers; stays, and goes;
It comes again; again takes flight;
And like a subtle presence grows,
And almost gathers into sight.

from

New Ballads

[1897]

SPRING SONG

About the flowerless land adventurous bees
  Pickeering hum; the rooks debate, divide,
  With many a hoarse aside,
  In solemn conclave on the budding trees;
  Larks in the skies and ploughboys o'er the leas
  Carol as if the winter ne'er had been;
  The very owl comes out to greet the sun;
  Rivers high-hearted run;
And hedges mantle with a flush of green.

The curlew calls me where the salt winds blow;
  His troubled note dwells mournfully and dies;
  Then the long echo cries
Deep in my heart. Ah, surely I must go.
For there the tides, moon-haunted, ebb and flow;
And there the seaboard murmurs resonant;
  The waves their interwoven fugue repeat
  And brooding surges beat
A slow, melodious, continual chant.

A NORTHERN SUBURB

Nature selects the longest way,
   And winds about in tortuous grooves;
A thousand years the oaks decay;
   The wrinkled glacier hardly moves.

But here the whetted fangs of change
   Daily devour the old demesne—
The busy farm, the quiet grange,
   The wayside inn, the village green.

In gaudy yellow brick and red,
   With rooting pipes, like creepers rank,
The shoddy terraces o'erspread
   Meadow, and garth, and daisied bank.

With shelves for rooms the houses crowd,
   Like draughty cupboards in a row—
Ice-chests when wintry winds are loud,
   Ovens when summer breezes blow.

Roused by the fee'd policeman's knock,
   And sad that day should come again,
Under the stars the workmen flock
   In haste to reach the workmen's train.

For here dwell those who must fulfil
   Dull tasks in uncongenial spheres,
Who toil through dread of coming ill,
   And not with hope of happier years—

The lowly folk who scarcely dare
   Conceive themselves perhaps misplaced,
Whose prize for unremitting care
   Is only not to be disgraced.

A WOMAN AND HER SON

'Has he come yet?' the dying woman asked.
'No,' said the nurse. 'Be quiet.'

              'When he comes
Bring him to me: I may not live an hour.'
'Not if you talk. Be quiet.'

              'When he comes

Bring him to me.'

                'Hush, will you!'

                    Night came down.
The cries of children playing in the street
Suddenly rose more voluble and shrill;
Ceased, and broke out again: and ceased and broke
In eager prate; then dwindled and expired.

'Across the dreary common once I saw
The moon rise out of London like a ghost.
Has the moon risen? Is he come?'

                'Not yet.
Be still, or you will die before he comes.'

The working-men with heavy iron tread,
The thin-shod clerks, the shopmen neat and plump
Home from the city came. On muddy beer
The melancholy mean suburban street
Grew maudlin for an hour; pianos waked
In dissonance from dreams of rusty peace,
And unpitched voices quavered tedious songs
Of sentiment infirm or nerveless mirth.

'Has he come yet?'
                                        'Be still or you will die!'

And when the hour of gaiety had passed,
And the poor revellers were gone to bed,
The moon among the chimneys wandering long
Escaped at last, and sadly overlooked
The waste raw land where doleful suburbs thrive.

Then came a firm quick step—measured but quick;
And then a triple knock that shook the house
And brought the plaster down.

                                        'My son!' she cried.
'Bring him to me!'

                                        He came; the nurse went out.

'Mother, I thought to spare myself this pain.'
He said at once, 'but that was cowardly.
And so I come to bid you try to think,
To understand at last.'

                                        'Still hard, my son?'
'Hard as the nether millstone.'

                                        'But I hope
To soften you,' she said, 'before I die.'

'And I to see you harden with a hiss
As life goes out in the cold bath of death.
Oh, surely now your creed will set you free
For one great moment, and the universe
Flash on your intellect as power, power, power,
Knowing not good or evil, God or sin,
But only everlasting yea and nay.
Is weakness greatness? No, a thousand times!

Is force the greatest? Yes, for ever yes!
Be strong, be great, now you have come to die.'

'My son, you seem to me a kind of prig.'

'How can I get it said? Think, mother, think!
Look back upon your fifty wretched years
And show me anywhere the hand of God.
Your husband saving souls—O, paltry souls
That need salvation!—lost the grip of things,
And left you penniless with none to aid
But me the prodigal. Back to the start!
An orphan girl, hurt, melancholy, frail,
Before you learned to play, your toil began:
That might have been your making, had the weight
Of drudgery, the unsheathed fire of woe
Borne down and beat on your defenceless life:
Souls shrivel up in these extremes of pain,
Or issue diamonds to engrave the world;
But yours before it could be made or marred,
Plucked from the burning, saved by faith, became
Inferior as a thing of paste that hopes
To pass for real in heaven's enduring[1] light.
You married then a crude evangelist,
Whose soul was like a wafer that can take
One single impress only.'

                    'Oh, my son!
Your father!'

                    'He, my father! These are times
When all must to the crucible—no thought,
Practice, or use, or custom sacro-sanct
But shall be violable now. And first
If ever we evade the wonted round,
The stagnant vortex of the eddying years,
The child must take the father by the beard,
And say, "What did you in begetting me?" '

---

[1] In Davidson's text the word 'enduing' is presumably a misprint.

'I will not listen!'

                          'But you shall, you must—
You cannot help yourself. Death in your eyes
And voice, and I to torture you with truth,
Even as your preachers for a thousand years
Pestered with falsehood souls of dying folk.
Look at the man, your husband. Of the soil;
Broad, strong, adust; head, massive; eyes of steel;
Yet some way ailing, for he understood
But one idea, and he married you.'

The dying woman sat up straight in bed;
A ghastly blush glowed on her yellow cheek,
And flame broke from her eyes, but words came not.

The son's pent wrath burnt on. 'He married you;
You were his wife, his servant; cheerfully
You bore him children; and your house was hell.
Unwell, half-starved, and clad in cast-off clothes,
We had no room, no sport; nothing but fear
Of our evangelist, whose little purse
Opened to all save us; who squandered smiles
On wily proselytes, and gloomed at home.
You had eight children; only three grew up;
Of these, one died bedrid, and one insane,
And I alone am left you. Think of it!
It matters nothing if a fish, a plant
Teem with waste offspring, but a conscious womb!
Eight times you bore a child, and in fierce throes,
For you were frail and small: of all your love,
Your hopes, your passion, not a memory steals
To smooth your dying pillow, only I
Am here to rack you. Where does God appear?'

'God shall appear,' the dying woman said.
'God has appeared: my heart is in his hand.

Were there no God, no Heaven!—Oh, foolish boy!
You foolish fellow! Pain and trouble here
Are God's benignest providence—the whip
And spur to Heaven. But joy was mine below—
I am unjust to God—great joy was mine:
Which makes Heaven sweeter too; because if earth
Afford such pleasure in mortality
What must immortal happiness be like!
Eight times I was a mother. Frail and small?
Yes; but the passionate, courageous mate
Of a strong man. Oh, boy! You paltry boy!
Hush! Think! Think—you! Eight times I bore a child,
Eight souls for God! In Heaven they wait for me—
My husband and the seven. I see them all!
And two are children still—my little ones!
While I have sorrowed here, shrinking sometimes
From that which was decreed, my Father, God,
Was storing Heaven with treasure for me. Hush!
My dowry in the skies! God's thoughtfulness!
I see it all! Lest Heaven might, unalloyed,
Distress my shy soul, I leave earth in doubt
Of your salvation: something to hope and fear
Until I get accustomed to the peace
That passeth understanding. When you come—
For you will come, my son. . . .'

                  Her strength gave out;
She sank down panting, bathed in tears and sweat.

'Could I but touch your intellect,' he cried,
'Before you die! Mother, the world is mad:
This castle in the air, this Heaven of yours,
Is the lewd dream of morbid vanity.
For each of us death is the end of all;
And when the sun goes out the race of men
Shall cease for ever. It is ours to make
This farce of fate a splendid tragedy:

Since we must be the sport of circumstance,
We should be sportsmen, and produce a breed
Of gallant creatures, conscious of their doom,
Marching with lofty brows, game to the last.
Oh good and evil, heaven and hell are lies!
But strength is great: there is no other truth:
This is the yea-and-nay that makes men hard.
Mother, be hard and happy in your death.'

'What do you say? I hear the waters roll . . .'
Then, with a faint cry, striving to arise—
'After I die I shall come back to you,
And then you must believe; you must believe,
For I shall bring you news of God and Heaven!'

He set his teeth, and saw his mother die.
Outside a city-reveller's tipsy tread
Severed the silence with a jagged rent;
The tall lamps flickered through the sombre street,
With yellow light hiding the stainless stars:
In the next house a child awoke and cried;
Far off a clank and clash of shunting trains
Broke out and ceased, as if the fettered world
Started and shook its irons in the night;
Across the dreary common citywards,
The moon, among the chimneys sunk again,
Cast on the clouds a shade of smoky pearl.

And when her funeral day had come, her son,
Before they fastened down the coffin lid,
Shut himself in the chamber, there to gaze
Upon her dead face, hardening his heart.
But as he gazed, into the smooth wan cheek
Life with its wrinkles shot again; the eyes
Burst open, and the bony fingers clutched
The coffin sides; the woman raised herself,
And owl-like in her shroud blinked on the light.

'Mother, what news of God and Heaven?' he asked.
Feeble and strange, her voice came from afar:
'I am not dead: I must have been asleep.'

'Do not imagine that. You lay here dead—
Three days and nights, a corpse. Life has come back:
Often it does, although faint-hearted folk
Fear to admit it: none of those who die,
And come to life again, can ever tell
Of any bourne from which they have returned:
Therefore they were not dead, your casuists say.
The ancient jugglery that tricks the world!
You lay here dead, three days and nights. What news?
"After I die I shall come back to you,
And then you must believe"—these were your words—
"For I shall bring you news of God and Heaven." '

She cast a look forlorn about the room:
The door was shut; the worn venetian, down;
And stuffy sunlight through the dusty slats
Spotted the floor, and smeared the faded walls.
He with his strident voice and eyes of steel
Stood by relentless.

                           'I remember, dear,'
She whispered, 'very little. When I died
I saw my children dimly bending down,
The little ones in front, to beckon me,
A moment in the dark; and that is all.'

'That was before you died—the last attempt
Of fancy to create the heart's desire.
Now mother, be courageous; now, be hard.'

'What must I say or do, my dearest son?
Oh me, the deep discomfort of my mind!
Come to me, hold me, help me to be brave,

And I shall make you happy if I can,
For I have none but you—none anywhere . . .
Mary, the youngest, whom you never saw
Looked out of Heaven first: her little hands . . .
Three days and nights, dead, and no memory! . . .
A poor old creature dying a second death,
I understand the settled treachery,
The plot of love and hope against the world.
Fearless, I gave myself at nature's call;
And when they died, my children, one by one,
All sweetly in my heart I buried them.
Who stole them while I slept? Where are they all?
My heart is eerie, like a rifled grave
Where silent spiders spin among the dust,
And the wind moans and laughs under its breath.
But in a drawer. . . . What is there in the drawer?
No pressure of a little rosy hand
Upon a faded cheek—nor anywhere
The seven fair stars I made. Oh love the cheat!
And hope, the radiant devil pointing up,
Lest men should cease to give the couple sport
And end the world at once! For three days dead—
Here in my coffin; and no memory!
Oh, it is hard! But I—I, too, am hard . . .
Be hard, my son, and steep your heart of flesh
In stony waters till it grows a stone,
Or love and hope will hack it with blunt knives
As long as it can feel.'

                    He, holding her,
With sobs and laughter spoke: his mind had snapped
Like a frayed string o'erstretched: 'Mother, rejoice;
For I shall make you glad. There is no heaven.
Your children are resolved to dust and dew:
But, mother, I am God. I shall create
The heaven of your desires. There must be heaven
For mothers and their babes. Let heaven be now!'

They found him conjuring chaos with mad words
And brandished hands across his mother's corpse.

Thus did he see her harden with a hiss
As life went out in the cold bath of death;
Thus did she soften him before she died:
For both were bigots—fateful souls that plague
The gentle world.

SUNSET

By down and shore the South-west bore
   The scent of hay, an airy load:
As if at fault it seemed to halt,
   Then, softly whispering, took the road,
To haunt the evening like a ghost,
Or some belated pilgrim lost.

High overhead the slow clouds sped;
   Beside the moon they furled their sails;
Soon in the skies their merchandise
   Of vapour, built in toppling bales,
Fulfilled a visionary pier
That spanned the eastern atmosphere.

Low in the west the sun addressed
   His courtship to the dark-browed night;
While images of molten seas,
   Of snowy slope and crimson height,
Of valleys dim and gulfs profound
Aloft a dazzling pageant wound.

Where shadows fell in glade and dell
   Uncovered shoulders nestled deep,
And here and there the braided hair
   Of rosy goddesses asleep;
For in a moment clouds may be
Dead, and instinct with deity.

A FROSTY MORNING

From heaven's high embrasure
   The sun with tufted rays
Illum'd the wandering azure
   And all the world's wide ways.

Usurping in its olden
   Abode the fog's demesne,
In watchet weeds and golden
   The still air sparkled keen.

On window-sill and door-post,
   On rail and tramway rust,
Embroidery of hoar-frost
   Was sewn like diamond dust.

Unthronged, or crowded densely
   By people business-led,
The pavements, tuned intensely,
   Rang hollow to the tread.

The traffic hurled and hammered
   Down every ringing street;
Like gongs the causeys clamoured,
   Like drums the asphalt beat.

While ruling o'er the olden
   Abode of fog unclean,
In watchet weeds and golden
   The still air sparkled keen.

'YOUNG POET AND OLD'

(*from* A Ballad of a Poet Born)

Upon a ruddy ember eve
　　They feasted in the hall:
The old broken man, with no one's leave,
　　Sat down among them all.

And while the swarthy rafters rang
　　With antique praise of wine,
There rose a conscious youth and sang
　　A ditty new and fine.

Of Fate's mills, and the human grist
　　They grind at, was his song;
He cursed the canting moralist
　　Who measures right and wrong.

'The earth, a flying tumour, wends
　　Through space all blotched and blown
With suns and worlds, with odds and ends
　　Of systems seamed and sewn:

'Beneath the sun it froths like yeast;
　　Its fiery essence flares;
It festers into man and beast;
　　It throbs with flowers and tares.

'Behold! 'tis but a heap of dust,
　　Kneaded by fire and flood;
While hunger fierce, and fiercer lust,
　　Drench it with tears and blood.

'Yet why seek after some new birth?
　　For surely, late or soon,
This ague-fit we call the earth
　　Shall be a corpse-cold moon.

'Why need we, lacking help and hope,
  By fears and fancies tossed,
Vainly debate with ruthless Fate,
  Fighting a battle lost?

'Fill high the bowl! We are the scum
  Of matter; fill the bowl;
Drink scathe to him, and death to him,
  Who dreams he has a soul.'

They clinked their cans and roared applause;
  The singer swelled with pride.
'You sneer and carp! Give me the harp,'
  The old man, trembling, cried.

They laughed and wondered, and grew still
  To see one so aghast
Smiting the chords; but all his skill
  Came back to him at last.

And lo, as searching-sweet as musk
  The words were and the tune,
And while he sang of dawn and dusk,
  Of midnight and of noon;

Of heaven and hell, of times and tides;
  Of wintry winds that blow,
Of spring that haunts the world and hides
  Her flowers among the snow;

Of Summer, rustling green and glad,
  With blossoms purfled fair;
Of autumn's wine-stained mouth and sad,
  Wan eyes, and golden hair;

Of Love, of Love, the wild sweet scent
  Of flowers, and words, and lives,
And loyal Nature's urgent bent
  Whereby the world survives;

Of magic Love that opes the ports
  Of sense and soul, that saith
The moonlight's meaning, and extorts
  The fealty of Death.

He sang of peace and work that bless
  The simple and the sage;
He sang of hope and happiness,
  He sang the Golden Age.

And the shamed listeners knew the spell
  That still enchants the years,
When the world's commonplaces fell
  In music on their ears.

from

The Last Ballad

[1899]

WAR SONG

In anguish we uplift
  A new unhallowed song:
The race is to the swift;
  The battle to the strong.

Of old it was ordained
  That we, in packs like curs,
Some thirty million trained
  And licensed murderers,

In crime should live and act,
  In cunning folk say sooth
Who flay the naked fact
  And carve the heart of truth.

The rulers cry aloud,
  'We cannot cancel war,
The end and bloody shroud
  Of wrongs the worst abhor,
And order's swaddling band:
  Know that relentless strife
Remains by sea and land
  The holiest law of life.
From fear in every guise,
  From sloth, from lust of pelf,
By war's great sacrifice
  The world redeems itself.
War is the source, the theme
  Of art; the goal, the bent

And brilliant academe
  Of noble sentiment;
The augury, the dawn
  Of golden times of grace;
The true catholicon,
  And blood-bath of the race.'

We thirty million trained
  And licensed murderers,
Like zanies rigged, and chained
  By drill and scourge and curse
In shackles of despair
  We know not how to break—
What do we victims care
  For art, what interest take
In things unseen, unheard?
  Some diplomat no doubt
Will launch a heedless word,
  And lurking war leap out!

We spell-bound armies then,
  Huge brutes in dumb distress,
Machines compact of men
  Who once had consciences,
Must trample harvests down—
  Vineyard, and corn and oil;
Dismantle town by town,
  Hamlet and homestead spoil
Of each appointed path,
  Till lust of havoc light
A blood-red blaze of wrath
  In every frenzied sight.

In many a mountain-pass,
  Or meadow green and fresh,
Mass shall encounter mass
  Of shuddering human flesh;

Opposing ordnance roar
  Across the swaths of slain,
And blood in torrents pour
  In vain—always in vain,
  For war breeds war again!

The shameful dream is past,
  The subtle maze untrod:
We recognize at last
  That war is not of God.
Wherefore we now uplift
  Our new unhallowed song:
The race is to the swift,
  The battle to the strong.

EARTH TO EARTH

Where the region grows without a lord,
　Between the thickets emerald-stoled,
In the woodland bottom the virgin sward,
　The cream of the earth, through depths of mold
　O'erflowing wells from secret cells,
While the moon and the sun keep watch and ward,
　And the ancient world is never old.

Here, alone, by the grass-green hearth
　Tarry a little: the mood will come!
Feel your body a part of earth;
　Rest and quicken your thought at home;
　Take your ease with the brooding trees;
Join in their deep-down silent mirth
　The crumbling rock and the fertile loam.

Listen and watch! The wind will sing;
　And the day go out by the western gate;
The night come up on her darkling wing;
　And the stars with flaming torches wait.
　Listen and see! And love and be
The day and the night and the world-wide thing
　Of strength and hope you contemplate.

No lofty Patron of Nature! No;
　Nor a callous devotee of Art!
But the friend and the mate of the high and the low,
　And the pal to take the vermin's part,
　Your inmost thought divinely wrought,
In the grey earth of your brain aglow
　With the red earth burning in your heart.

Scales of pearly cloud inlay
   North and south the turquoise sky,
While the diamond lamp of day
   Quenchless burns, and time on high
A moment halts upon his way
   Bidding noon again good-bye.

Gaffers, gammers, huzzies, louts,
   Couples, gangs, and families
Sprawling, shake, with Babel-shouts
   Bluff King Hal's funereal trees;
And eddying groups of stare-abouts
   Quiz the sandstone Hercules.

When their tongues and tempers tire,
   Harry and his little lot
Condescendingly admire
   Lozenge-bed and crescent-plot,
Aglow with links of azure fire,
   Pansy and forget-me-not.

Where the emerald shadows rest
   In the lofty woodland aisle,
Chaffing lovers quaintly dressed
   Chase and double many a mile,
Indifferent exiles in the west
   Making love in cockney style.

Now the echoing palace fills;
   Men and women, girls and boys
Trample past the swords and frills,
   Kings and Queens and trulls and toys;
Or listening loll on window-sills,
   Happy amateurs of noise!

That for pictured rooms of state!
   Out they hurry, wench and knave,
Where beyond the palace-gate
   Dusty legions swarm and rave,
With laughter, shriek, inane debate,
   Kentish fire and comic stave.

Voices from the river call;
   Organs hammer tune on tune;
Larks triumphant over all
   Herald twilight coming soon,
For as the sun begins to fall
   Near the zenith gleams the moon.

IN THE ISLE OF DOGS

While the water-wagon's ringing showers
Sweetened the dust with a woodland smell,
'Past noon, past noon, two sultry hours,'
Drowsily fell
From the schoolhouse clock
In the Isle of Dogs by Millwall Dock.

Mirrored in shadowy windows draped
With ragged net or half-drawn blind
Bowsprits, masts, exactly shaped
To woo or fight the wind,
Like monitors of guilt
By strength and beauty sent,
Disgraced the shameful houses built
To furnish rent.

From the pavements and the roofs
In shimmering volumes wound
The wrinkled heat;
Distant hammers, wheels and hoofs,
A turbulent pulse of sound,
Southward obscurely beat,
The only utterance of the afternoon,
Till on a sudden in the silent street
An organ-man drew up and ground
The Old Hundredth tune.

Forthwith the pillar of cloud that hides the past
Burst into flame,
Whose alchemy transmuted house and mast,
Street, dockyard, pier and pile:
By magic sound the Isle of Dogs became
A northern isle—
A green isle like a beryl set

In a wine-coloured sea,
Shadowed by mountains where a river met
The ocean's arm extended royally.

There also in the evening on the shore
An old man ground the Old Hundredth tune,
An old enchanter steeped in human lore,
Sad-eyed, with whitening beard, and visage lank:
Not since and not before,
Under the sunset or the mellowing moon,
Has any hand of man's conveyed
Such meaning in the turning of a crank.

Sometimes he played
As if his box had been
An organ in an abbey richly lit;
For when the dark invaded day's demesne,
And the sun set in crimson and in gold;
When idlers swarmed upon the esplanade,
And a late steamer wheeling towards the quay
Struck founts of silver from the darkling sea,
The solemn tune arose and shook and rolled
Above the throng,
Above the hum and tramp and bravely knit
All hearts in common memories of song.

Sometimes he played at speed;
Then the Old Hundredth like a devil's mass
Instinct with evil thought and evil deed,
Rang out in anguish and remorse. Alas!
That men must know both Heaven and Hell!
Sometimes the melody
Sang with the murmuring surge;
And with the winds would tell
Of peaceful graves and of the passing bell.
Sometimes it pealed across the bay

A high triumphal dirge,
A dirge
For the departing undefeated day.

A noble tune, a high becoming mate
Of the capped mountains and the deep broad firth;
A simple tune and great,
The fittest utterance of the voice of earth.

AFTERNOON

The hostess of the sky, the moon,
   Already stoops to entertain
The golden light of afternoon,
   And the wan earthshine from the plain.

No rustling wings, no voices warp
   The ripened stillness of the day;
Behind the Downs the sheltered thorpe
   Expectant overhangs the way.

What laughter, whisper, sigh or groan,
   A hazardous, a destined sound,
Shall first usurp the airy throne
   Where silence rules with twilight crowned?

Hark! hark! an antique noise! Across
   The road the bellows fires anew
With jar and sough the hissing dross,
   Close-raked about the half-wrought shoe.

From the swart chimney lilac smoke,
   The blacksmith's prayer, to heaven ascends;
The hammers double stroke on stroke;
   The stubborn iron sparkling bends.

Then voices near and far break out;
   The starlings in the tree-tops scold;
The larks against each other shout;
   The blackbirds scatter pearl and gold;

The jackdaws prate; the cuckoos call;
   And shrill enough to reach the spheres
Resounds the brazen madrigal
   Of half a hundred chanticleers.

WAITING

Within unfriendly walls
 We starve—or starve by stealth.
Oxen fatten in their stalls;
 You guard the harrier's health:
They never can be criminals.
 And can't compete for wealth.
  From the mansion and the palace
  Is there any help or hail
  For the tenants of the alleys,
   Of the workhouse and the jail?

Though lands await our toil,
 And earth half-empty rolls,
Cumberers of English soil,
 We cringe for orts and doles—
Prosperity's accustomed foil,
 Millions of useless souls.
  In the gutters and the ditches
   Human vermin festering lurk—
  We, the rust upon your riches;
  We, the flaw in all your work.

Come down from where you sit;
 We look to you for aid.
Take us from the miry pit,
 And lead us undismayed:
Say, 'Even you, outcast, unfit,
 Forward with sword and spade!'
  And myriads of us idle
   Would thank you through our tears,
  Though you drove us with a bridle,
  And a whip about our ears!

From cloudy cape to cape
  The teeming waters seethe;
Golden grain and purple grape
  The regions overwreathe.
Will no one help us to escape?
  We scarce have room to breathe.
    You might try to understand us:
      We are waiting night and day
For a captain to command us,
  And the word we must obey.

The Testament of a Man Forbid

[1901]

Mankind has cast me out. When I became
So close a comrade of the day and night,
Of earth and of the seasons of the year,
And so submissive in my love of life
And study of the world that I unknew
The past and names renowned, religion, art,
Inventions, thoughts, and deeds, as men unknow
What good and evil fate befell their souls
Before their bodies gave them residence,
(How the old letter haunts the spirit still!
As if the soul were other than the sum
The body's powers make up—a golden coin,
Amount of so much silver, so much bronze!)
I said, rejoicing, 'Now I stand erect,
And am that which I am.' Compassionate
I watched a motley crowd beside me bent
Beneath unsteady burdens, toppling loads
Of volumes, news and lore antique, that showered
About their ears to be re-edified
On aching heads and shoulders overtasked.
Yet were these hodmen cheerful, ignorant
Of woe whose character it is to seem
Predestined and an honourable care:
They read their books, re-read, and read again;
They balanced libraries upon their polls,
And tottered through the valley almost prone,

But certain they were nobler than the beasts.
I saw besides in fields and cities hordes
Of haggard people soaked in filth and slime
Wherewith they fed the jaded earth the while
Their souls of ordure stank; automata
That served machines whose tyrannous revolt
Enthralled their lords, as if the mistletoe
Displaying mournful gold and wintry pearls
On sufferance, should enchant the forest oak
To be its accident and parasite;
Wretches and monsters that were capable
Of joy and sorrow once, their bodies numbed,
Their souls deflowered, their reason disendowed
By noisome trades, or at the furnaces,
In drains and quarries and the sunless mines;
And myriads upon myriads, human still
Without redemption drudging till they died.

Aware how multitudes of those enslaved
No respite sought, but squandered leisure hours
Among the crowd whose choice or task it was
To balance libraries upon their polls,
I laughed a long low laugh with weeping strung,
A rosary of tears, to see mankind
So dauntless and so dull, and cried at last,
'Good people, honest people, cast them off
And stand erect, for few are helped by books.
What! will you die crushed under libraries?
Lo! thirty centuries of literature
Have curved your spines and overborne your brains!
Off with it—all of it! Stand up; behold
The earth; life, death, and day and night!
Think not the things that have been said of these;
But watch them and be excellent, for men
Are what they contemplate.'
                              They mocked me: 'Yah!
The fox who lost his tail! Though you are crazed

We have our wits about us.'
                                        'Nay,' I cried;
'There was besides an ape who lost his tail
That he might change to man. Undo the past!
The rainbow reaches Asgard now no more;
Olympus stands untenanted; the dead
Have their serene abode in earth itself,
Our womb, our nurture, and our sepulchre.
Expel the sweet imaginings, profound
Humanities and golden legends, forms
Heroic, beauties, tripping shades, embalmed
Through hallowed ages in the fragrant hearts
And generous blood of men; the climbing thoughts
Whose roots ethereal grope among the stars,
Whose passion-flowers perfume eternity,
Weed out and tear, scatter and tread them down;
Dismantle and dilapidate high heaven!
It has been said: Ye must be born again.
I say to you: Men must be that they are.
Philosophy, the juggling dupe who finds
Astounding meanings in the Universe,
Commodiously secreted by himself;
Religion, that appoints the soul a flight
Empyreal—hoods its vision then and plucks
Its plumes, its arching pinions tethers down
To flap about a laystall; Art sublime,
The ancient harlot of the ages, she
Whose wig of golden tinct, enamelled face
And cushioned bosom rivet glowing looks,
Whose scented flatulence diviner seems
Than dulcet breath of girls who keep their trysts
In hawthorn brakes devoutly, when the sap
Bestirs the troubled forest and the winds
Solace the moonlit earth with whispered news:
Religion, Art, Philosophy—this God,
This Beauty, this Idea men have filled
The world with, study still, and still adore,

Are only segments of the spirit's tail
We must outgrow, if spirit would ascend,
(Let Spirit be the word for body-and-soul!
Will language ne'er be fused and forged anew?)
And quit the withering life of fear and shame,
Of agony and pitiful desire
To reign untailed in heaven hereafter—Laugh!
The changing image seizes you. Or thus:
This Beauty, this Divinity, this Thought,
This hallowed bower and harvest of delight
Whose roots ethereal seemed to clutch the stars,
Whose amaranths perfumed eternity,
Is fixed in earthly soil enriched with bones
Of used-up workers; fattened with the blood
Of prostitutes, the prime manure; and dressed
With brains of madmen and the broken hearts
Of children. Understand it, you at least
Who toil all day and writhe and groan all night
With roots of luxury, a cancer struck
In every muscle: out of you it is
Cathedrals rise and Heaven blossoms fair;
You are the hidden putrefying source
Of beauty and delight, of leisured hours,
Of passionate loves and high imaginings;
You are the dung that keeps the roses sweet.
I say, uproot it; plough the land; and let
A summer-fallow sweeten all the World.'

With mud bespattered, bruised with staves and stoned—
'You called us dung!'—me from their midst they drove.
Alone I went in darkness and in light,
Colour and sound attending on my steps,
And Life and death, the ministers of men,
My constant company. But in my heart
Of hearts I longed for human neighbourhood,
And bent my pride to win men back again.
I came, a penitent; and on my knees

I climbed their stairs; I thundered at their doors,
And cried, 'I am your brother; in your wrath,
As brethren should, destroy me; at your hands
I must have life or death: I cannot bear
The outcast's fate.'
                                    They bade me then proclaim
How seemed the World now in my penitence.
But when I rose to speak, their palaces,
Their brothels, slums, cathedrals, theatres,
Asylums, factories, exchanges, banks,
The patched-up world of heirlooms, hand-me-downs
That worm and moth dispute, of make-believe,
Of shoddy, pinchbeck, sweepings of the street,
Of war disguised, of unconcealed chicane,
Of shrivelled drudge and swollen parvenu,
Turned at my glance into that murky vale
Where patient hodmen on their rounded backs
Sustained the thought of thirty centuries,
Where multitudes of slaves renounced their rest
To balance libraries upon their polls;
Or to that giant oaf (for vision shifts
The world about like winds that shape the clouds)
Whose spiritual tail, most awkward now
That breeches hide the rump, is cherished still
With ursine piety; or to that bower
Of Heaven's Delight whose barbed and cancerous roots
Are struck in earthly soil enriched with blood
Of men and women. As I saw I said:
(How could I else!) and bade them as before
'Arise! Uproot the pleasance; plough the land,
And let the World lie fallow. Only then
Can any seed of change have room to grow.'
They yelled upon me and their missiles flew;
But one arose to represent the World,
And at his nod their clamour ceased. He said:
'There is no harbour here for such as you.
You know not what you say nor understand

How you have hurt yourself. You cannot—fool,
And answered as befits!—contrive to make
A monkey human by caudatomy;
Nor can humanity transcend itself
By shearing off its spirit at the root.
That of the tail is false analogy.
Man springs from out the past: his tap-roots pierce
The strata of the ages, drawing strength
From every generation, every cult.
The scission of the smallest rootlet harms
His growth.'

               Then turning he adjured the crowd:
'Be warned or be accursed! This monster steps
Beyond the scope and furthest bound of man:
Mere mirror is his brain; his heart, mere husk.
A waft of death comes from him. Would you live
Indifferent to your own delight, unmoved
By kindred sorrow, and oblivious
Of all your fathers did, then give him ear,
And quit forever the resourceful past.
I know you will not. What! Some pause to think?
Resort now to the knife and you will find
'Tis not an unbecoming, useless tail
You sever manfully to be yourselves,
But suicide of soul that you commit.'

To me: 'You ask for life or death from us,
Because you cannot bear the outcast's fate.
We disregard your claim: what you can bear
Is no concern of ours: we cast you out.
Your well-earned portion of the Universe
Is isolation and eternal death.
Cut off, an alien, here you have no home:
No face shall ever gladden at your step,
No woman long to see you. Get you hence,
And seek the desert; or since your soul is dead,

120

Return your body to the earth at once,
And let resolved oblivion triumph now.'

Gladly the World approved with hand and voice;
And one, a woman, offered me a knife:
'And let resolved oblivion triumph now,'
She echoed. Had it been my will to die,
I should not then have made the sacrifice
At the World's bidding; but I chose to live,
For while I live the victory is mine.

So I went forth for evermore forbid
The company of men. The Universe,
Systems and suns and all that breathes and is,
Appeared at first in that dread solitude
Only the momentary, insolent
Irruption of a glittering fantasy
Into the silent, empty Infinite.
But eyes and ears were given to me again:
With these a man may do; with these, endure.

I haunt the hills that overlook the sea.
Here in the Winter like a meshwork shroud
The sifted snow reveals the perished land,
And powders wisps of knotgrass dank and dead
That trail like faded locks on mouldering skulls
Unearthed from shallow burial. With the Spring
The west-wind thunders through the budding hedge
That stems the furrowed steep—a sound of drums,
Of gongs and muted cymbals; yellow breasts
And brown wings whirl in gusts, fly chaffering, drop,
And surge in gusts again; in wooded coombs
The hyacinth with purple diapers
The russet beechmast, and the cowslips hoard
Their virgin gold in lucent chalices;
The sombre furze, all suddenly attired
In rich brocade, the enterprise in chief

And pageant of the season, overrides
The rolling land and girds the bosomed plain
That strips her green robe to a saffron shore
And steps into the surf where threads and scales
And arabesques of blue and emerald wave
Begin to damascene the iron sea;
While faint from upland fold and covert peal
The sheep-bell and the cuckoo's mellow chime.
Then when the sovereign light from which we came,
Of earth enamoured, bends most questioning looks,
I watch the land grow beautiful, a bride
Transfigured with desire of her great lord.
Betrothal-music of the tireless larks,
Heaven-high, heaven-wide possesses all the air,
And wreathes the shining lattice of the light
With chaplets, purple clusters, vintages
Of sound from the first fragrant breath and first
Tear-sprinkled blush of Summer to the deep
Transmuted fire, the smouldering golden moons,
The wine-stained dusk of Autumn harvest-ripe;
And I behold the period of Time,
When Memory shall devolve and Knowledge lapse
Wanting a subject, and the willing earth
Leap to the bosom of the sun to be
Pure flame once more in a new time begun:
Here, as I pace the pallid doleful hills
And serpentine declivities that creep
Unhonoured to the ocean's shifting verge,
Or where with prouder curve and greener sward,
Surmounting peacefully the restless tides,
The cliffed escarpment ends in stormclad strength.

from

A Rosary

[1903]

THE WASTREL

An eyesore to the tourist on the shoulder of the knock
  Above the green-fledged larches where the squirrel keeps its
                     house,
The pale dissenting chapel, like a pharos on a rock,
  With strong, pathetic preaching that the very dead might
                     rouse,
Was lighted for an hour and twenty minutes by the clock,
  While the cushats moaned and muttered deep among the
                     rustling boughs.

With Conybeare-and-Howson[1] laid on thick for local hue,
  And Meyer's and Lange's[2] comments to elucidate the text,
The minister exhibited a panoramic view
Of the story of the wastrel and the father that he vext:
Of little but his Bible and his creed the preacher knew,
  And dogma like a razor his emotions had unsexed.

Then came the modern instance, and the congregation stirred,
  And scrutinized the pew in which the preacher's family sat,
'I knew it,' thought each member, 'at the very opening word!'
  And felt as perspicacious as a dog that smells a rat:
The preacher's wife and daughters seized their Bibles where
                     they heard,
And his son, as red as poppies, stooped and glanced at this
                     and that.

'But recently,' the preacher said, 'to London town there went
  A youth from our vicinity against his father's wish;
To make a fortune—honestly, if possible—he meant,

[1] *Life and Epistles of St Paul*, W. J. Conybeare and J. S. Howson (1852).
[2] *Commentary on the Old and New Testament*, H. W. Meyer; *Commentary on the Old and New Testaments*, edited by J. P. Lange.

Forgetting quite how God examines both sides of the dish:
Unless a holy life exhale to Heaven a savoury scent,
  We know how very profitless the loaves are and the fish . . .'

The wife and daughters shrivel up and shut their eyes and cry
  As the preacher drives the lancet home and lays their heart-
                                        strings bare;
But the wastrel, cool and clammy, feels a wind of pride go by,
  And hears his pulses clank above monition, praise and
                                        prayer—
'Oho, for London Town again, where folk in peace can die,
  And the thunder-and-lightning devil of a train that takes
                                        me there.'

from

The Testament of a
Prime Minister

[1904]

A VISION OF JUDGMENT'

(*from* The Testament Of A Prime Minister)

                  . . . The trump
Of doom exhaled a long-enduring sigh,
A sigh, no louder, heard and felt throughout
The quaking earth; and in the zenith reared,
The great white throne and Him that sat thereon
Illumined space insufferably bright.
Against His glance the star-strewn firmament,
As evanescent as a wreath of mist
At sunrise, perished utterly. The dead
Before the throne awaited judgement. Books
Were opened and another book which is
The book of life; and all the dead were judged
Out of the matters written in the books
According to their actions. On the right,
When the eternal sentence was pronounced,
I saw the great ones of the earth appear
Magnificently confident of heaven—
The kings, the conquerors, the wise, the bold.
The rich, the proud, and all the lusty lives
That took their power and pleasure in the world
'Enter, ye blessèd, enter!'—from the throne
The high decree. 'Inherit now the realm
Prepared for you from the beginning, ye
That used the world I made superb in strength,
Unparagoned in beauty—ye that loved
The haughty morning and the radiant night,
That stored the brilliant hours with generous strife,

With sweet repose, with passion, and with joy,
Glorying and revelling in the gifts I gave.
Created of the self-same stuff as I,
And all My suns and systems, Matter, strained
From the great staple of the Universe
Throughout millenniums of elaborate choice,
Conscious, self-conscious, free to know, to think,
To do, all ye that had my world in charge,
And set yourselves to fill it with delight,
With noble wars, with beauty and with wealth,
With hope for man, with hope for life, with life,
And ever and always life, partake with Me
To all eternity the joys of heaven.'

Upon the left—shuddering I saw it so—
The Son of Man and His elect appeared,
Apostles, martyrs, votarists, virgins, saints.
The poor in spirit, the mourners and the meek,
And they that hungered after righteousness,
The merciful and all the pure in heart,
Peacemakers and the salt of the earth I saw
Upon the left in sore amazement stand.
'Depart from Me, ye cursëd'—from the throne
The dread decree—'into eternal fire;
Deniers, slanderers, fools that turned to scorn
The perfect world I made superb in strength,
Unparagoned in beauty; ye that stained
The haughty morning and the radiant night,
Seasons and tides with liturgies and forms,
With cries and intercessions, prayers and tears,
Ashamed to use the glory I had given;
Ye rancorous poisoners of life that found
Temptation only where I offered joy,
My splendid world a charnel-house, and Me
A God of infelicity and woe,
A God of everything unfit to live,
Hating My gifts of intellect, of pride,

Of strength and freedom. Of the self-same stuff
As I and all My suns and galaxies,
The purest Matter, sifted forth and strained
From the great staple of the Universe
Throughout millenniums of elaborate choice,
Conscious, self-conscious, free to know, to think
To do, having My world in charge, ye set
Yourselves to drain it of delight, of love,
Of beauty, passion, power, supplied the void
With lust, revenge, distress, corruption, hate,
And made My will to life a will to death.
Ye hypocrites, that with a holy lie
Tarnished the cleanliness immaculate
Of human generation, soiling life
On to the end from his pellucid fount
And origin divine, beholding earth
A leprous crust of Sin, depart from Me
Into eternal fire prepared for them
That make my will to live a will to die.'

from

Holiday and Other Poems

[1906]

A RUNNABLE STAG

When the pods went pop on the broom, green broom,
  And apples began to be golden-skinned,
We harboured a stag in the Priory coomb,
  And we feathered his trail up-wind, up-wind,
  We feathered his trail up-wind—
    A stag of warrant, a stag, a stag,
    A runnable stag, a kingly crop,
    Brow, bay and tray and three on top,
    A stag, a runnable stag.

Then the huntsman's horn rang yap, yap, yap,
  And 'Forwards' we heard the harbourer shout;
But 'twas only a brocket that broke a gap
  In the beechen underwood, driven out,
  From the underwood antlered out
    By warrant and might of the stag, the stag,
    The runnable stag, whose lordly mind
    Was bent on sleep, though beamed and tined
    He stood, a runnable stag.

So we tufted the covert till afternoon
  With Tinkerman's Pup and Bell-of-the-North;
And hunters were sulky and hounds out of tune
  Before we tufted the right stag forth,
  Before we tufted him forth,
    The stag of warrant, the wily stag,
    The runnable stag with his kingly crop,
    Brow, bay and tray and three on top,
    The royal and runnable stag.

It was Bell-of-the-North and Tinkerman's Pup
  That stuck to the scent till the copse was drawn.
'Tally ho! tally ho!' and the hunt was up,
  The tufters whipped and the pack laid on,
  The resolute pack laid on,
    And the stag of warrant away at last,
    The runnable stag, the same, the same,
    His hoofs on fire, his horns like flame,
    A stag, a runnable stag.

'Let your gelding be: if you check or chide
He stumbles at once and you're out of the hunt;
For three hundred gentlemen, able to ride,
  On hunters accustomed to bear the brunt,
  Accustomed to bear the brunt,
    Are after the runnable stag, the stag,
    The runnable stag with his kingly crop,
    Brow, bay and tray and three on top,
    The right, the runnable stag.'

By perilous paths in coomb and dell,
  The heather, the rocks, and the river-bed,
The pace grew hot, for the scent lay well,
  And a runnable stag goes right ahead,
  The quarry went right ahead—

Ahead, ahead, and fast and far;
His antlered crest, his cloven hoof,
Brow, bay and tray and three aloof,
The stag, the runnable stag.

For a matter of twenty miles and more,
  By the densest hedge and the highest wall,
Through herds of bullocks he baffled the lore
  Of harbourer, huntsman, hounds and all,
  Of harbourer, hounds and all—
    The stag of warrant, the wily stag,
    For twenty miles, and five and five,
    He ran, and he never was caught alive,
    This stag, this runnable stag.

When he turned at bay in the leafy gloom,
  In the emerald gloom where the brook ran deep,
He heard in the distance the rollers boom,
  And he saw in a vision of peaceful sleep,
  In a wonderful vision of sleep,
    A stag of warrant, a stag, a stag,
    A runnable stag in a jewelled bed,
    Under the sheltering ocean dead,
    A stag, a runnable stag.

So a fateful hope lit up his eye,
  And he opened his nostrils wide again,
And he tossed his branching antlers high
  As he headed the hunt down the Charlock glen,
  As he raced down the echoing glen,
    For five miles more, the stag, the stag,
    For twenty miles, and five and five,
    Not to be caught now, dead or alive,
    The stag, the runnable stag.

Three hundred gentlemen, able to ride,
   Three hundred horses as gallant and free,
Behind him escape on the evening tide,
   Far out till he sank in the Severn Sea,
   Till he sank in the depths of the sea—
     The stag, the buoyant stag, the stag
     That slept at last in a jewelled bed
   Under the sheltering ocean spread,
   The stag, the runnable stag.

APPLE-TREES

When autumn stains and dapples
The diverse land,
Thickly studded with apples
The apple-trees stand.

Their mystery none discovers,
So none can tell—
Not the most passionate lovers
Of garth and fell;
For the silent sunlight weaves
The orchard spell,
Bough, bole, and root,
Mysterious, hung with leaves,
Embossed with fruit.

Though merle and throstle were loud,
Silent *their* passion in spring,
A blush of blossom wild-scented;
And now when no song-birds sing,
They are heavy with apples and proud
And supremely contented—
All fertile and green and sappy,
No wish denied,
Exceedingly quiet and happy
And satisfied!

No jealousy, anger, or fashion
Of strife
Perturbs in their stations
The apple-trees. Life
Is an effortless passion,
Fruit, bough, and stem,
A beautiful patience
For them.

Frost of the harvest-moon
Changes their sap to wine;
Ruddy and golden soon
Their clustered orbs will shine,
By favour
Of many a wind,
Of morn and noon and night,
Fulfilled from core to rind
With savour
Of all delight.

EPPING FOREST—NOVEMBER

Woods and coppices by tempest lashed;
   Pollard shockheads glaring in the rain;
Jet-black underwood with crimson splashed—
   Rich November, one wet crimson stain!

Turf that whispered moistly to the tread;
   Bursts of laughter from the shuffled leaves;
Pools of light in distant arbours spread;
   Depths of darkness under forest eaves.

High above the wind the clouds at rest
   Emptied every vat and steeply hurled
Reservoirs and floods; the wild nor'west
   Raked the downpour ere it reached the world;

Part in wanton sport and part in ire,
   Flights of rain on ruddy foliage rang:
Woven showers like sheets of silver fire
   Streamed; and all the forest rocked and sang.

YULETIDE

Now wheel and hoof and horn
In every street
Stunned to its chimney-tops,
In every murky street—
Each lamp-lit gorge by traffic rent
Asunder,
Ravines of serried shops
By business tempests torn—
In every echoing street,
From early morn
Till jaded night falls dead,
Wheel, hoof, and horn
Tumultuous thunder
Beat
Under
A noteless firmament
Of lead.

When the winds list
A fallen cloud
Where yellow dregs of light
Befouled remain,
The woven gloom
Of smoke and mist,
The soot-entangled rain
That jumbles day and night
In city and town,
An umber-emerald shroud
Rehearsing doom,
The London fog comes down.
But sometimes silken beams,
As bright
As adamant on fire,
Of the uplifted sun's august attire,
With frosty fibrous light

Magnetic shine
Of happier dreams
That abrogate despair,
When all the sparkling air
Of smoke and sulphur shriven,
Like an iced wine
Fills the high cup
Of heaven;
For urban park and lawn,
The city's scenery,
Heaths, commons, dells
That compass London rich
In greenery,
With diamond-dust of rime
Empowdered, flash
At dawn;
And tossing bells
Of stealthy hansoms chime
With silvery crash
In radiant ways
Attuned and frozen up
To concert pitch—
In resonant ways,
Where wheels and hoofs inwrought,
Cars, omnibuses, wains,
Beat, boom, and clash
Discordant fugal strains
Of cymbals, trumpets, drums;
While careless to arrive,
The nerved pedestrian comes
Exulting in the splendour overhead,
And in the live
Elastic ground,
The pavement, tense and taut,
That yields a twangling sound
At every tread.

'A THRENODY CELEBRATING THE FALL OF THE LEAF'

(from Bartlemas[1]*)*

No longer the nightingales chant
 To the silvery pulses of night,
That echo the measure and grant
 Responsal of starry delight:
No nightingales longer descant
 To the stars as they throb with delight
Of the passionate answer they grant
 The music that troubles the night—
As they vibrate and bloom with delight
 In the hanging gardens of night.
For the silences, harvested, throng,
 Though the gold and purpureal dye—
 Though the lacquer, the mordant, and dye
Of the autumn, like sounds of a song
 Into colour transmutable, lie
On the Forest—the crystalline tune
 That the spheres were imagined to play
Into colour transformed in the noon
 Of an ever adventurous day;
Above and within and about,
 The perfected silences throng—
In the Forest the silences throng:
No throstle, no blackbird devout
 As the seraphim mingle their song,
With perfume entangle the light
 And powder the woodland with pearl,
Nor usher the star-stricken night
With incense and melody rare;
 The song-thrush devout and the merle
No longer enrapture the air
 With concord of ruby and pearl;

---

[1] Davidson so described this passage in his essay 'On Poetry', printed at the back of 'Holiday and Other Poems'.

Nor now can the nightingale sing
 Expecting a stellar reply;
No fugues intergarlanded ring
 Of the earth and the clusters on high—
Sidereal echoes that bring
 The crystalline tears and the sigh
For the end of a beautiful thing
 That soldered the earth and the sky.

'NELSON'

(*from* Our Day)

A fragile form,
The delicate sheath of valour absolute;
Ambition, daring, honour, constancy,
Prescience, dominion, passion, scope, design,
A woman's tenderness, an infant's awe,
An adamantine courage, mercy, power
Attuned and fateful in an invalid!
Sea-lord, sea-god, his clear, transcendent love
Endowed his friends with lustre of his own,
And saw no blemish for excess of light
Which his great spirit shed: his glittering scorn,
His hate for England's sake of England's foes,
Diviner than his love, at England's need
O'erthrew the splendid Titan who essayed
To wrest the loyal sea from English hands,
Holding in trust that greatest gift of Fate.
The Nile, the Baltic, saw his pregnant war;
The palsied navies shrivelled at his touch;
So suddenly he came, so swiftly smote,
So wholly conquered, that his deeds remain
The bulwark maritime of England's power.
Nothing could tame his soul: that ocean-hunt
About the Atlantic and about in quest
Of action France and Spain denied,
Whetted his lust of battle; long delay,
That withers enterprise and rots desire
Even of enduring things, augmented all
His purpose and matured the valiant seed
Of utmost victory. Wherefore upon the dawn
Foreknown of battle—for the Admiral said
'The twenty-first will be our day'—he paced
His quarter-gallery subtly clad already
In the shadow of his glory; prepossessed
Besides with death; and like a spirit calm

That treads the threshold of eternity.
Now, when the morning brimmed the western world,
And on the weather-gleam a headland rose
Assured of fame, and the confederate fleets
Appeared between, hull crowding hull, five miles
Of armament, our great sea-warrior bade
The battle be. Southward the ships of France,
The ships of Spain, northward the English sailed,
As if they meant to pass each other by
In some majestic ritual of the tide.
But Nelson's signals, winged like thought aloft,
Undid that minuet! Twelve sail of his,
The weather line, with Collingwood to lee,
Bore up amain—the wind west by nor'-west——
And eastward stood athwart the banded fleets,
That veered unwieldily and headed north
With safe retreat on Cadiz, till Nelson's touch
Precipitated battle—he on their van
And Collingwood against their southern flank:
Two columns opportunely; yet to the end
The sailing order held the battle-line—
Our Admiral's prophecy and inspired device.
That happy signal first: 'England expects
That every man will do his duty'; then
Drums beat to quarters: gunners, stripped and girt,
The naked flesh of England against the fire
And rending bolt of England's foes, unlashed
Their ordnance: frowning crews, equipped
With linstock, priming-iron, rammer, wad,
Crowbar and handspike, cartridge, wreaths of shot,
Stood by each carronade, each red-lipped gun;
Topman and boarder, trimmer, musketeer,
Marine and powder-boy fulfilled his post,
His deed, his errand, transfigured suddenly.
The ceremonial wind controlled the approach,
Keeping a pageant-pace; and towering sails
Of England's navy, sheeted to the sky,

Slumbered at ease, a dulcet, virgin sleep,
So placid in their bosoms the breath of heaven
Dwelt like a dream, as every vessel, groomed
For war and marshalled on the vagrant surge
Of coming tempest, rode to victory.
France fired the nuptial gun; the flags broke out
Of every nation, and the battle joined.
In front of England the *Royal Sovereign* first
Achieved the enemy's range. The *Victory* next,
Silent against a navy's broadsides, forged
Ahead; and when her double-shotted guns,
One after one, at twenty feet had ploughed
The *Bucentaure* endlong, aboard the doomed
Redoubtable she ran. Forthwith amid
The din of cannon against cannon, mouth
To bellowing mouth, the shriek of timber crashed
And rent, the thund'rous voice of men absorbed
In the wild trance and waking dream of war,
Carnage and agony and the rhythmic swing
And travail of the deed, as Nelson paced
His quarter-deck awaiting the superb,
Unmatched event his genius had ordained,
The fatal marksman in the enemy's top
Espied his honours and England's hero fell.
Down in the winepress of the war where blood
O'erflowed the orlop, where the wounded strewed
The noisome cockpit and the grimy sweat
Cooled on the labouring surgeons, Nelson died:
The swarthy smoke that coiled from poop to hold
Obscured the glimmering lanterns; overhead
The cannon leapt; like a taut rope the hull
Quivered from stem to stern with every shot;
And still above the thunder of the strife,
Cresting the uproar, pealed the great hurrah
Of all the English crews, as ship by ship
The baffled navies struck and Nelson's name
Became immortal.

from

The Triumph of Mammon

[1907]

from THE TRIUMPH OF MAMMON

The atheist Mammon, who has gained the throne of Thule by murdering his father and his brother, means to reform the kingdom according to his own image. He receives in audience the leaders of 'the principal factions which in our time divide opinion in Thule, viz.: Socialists, calling themselves Reformers; Neo-pagans who desire the restoration of Rome mythology as a living faith; and the Inceptors of the Teutonic Religion, who deem the time ripe for the evolution of a New God'.

Mammon: Thrice welcome, Master Mayor. Now let me see:
(*Sits and consults the Mayor's petition.*)
'Inceptors of a new religion': come!
Your businesses, municipal affairs,
Your families, prospects, pleasures, sickness,
       health—
Are not these all you need?

Larum: Oh no, King Mammon!
In times and tides of happiness and woe
We must give thanks, we must solicit strength:
The soul of man subsists in prayer and praise.

Mammon: Now, I remember: you are nonconformist,
Proud of a purer creed, a broader mind.

Larum: Loathing a dead creed and a narrow mind.

Mammon: All creeds must die: why have a creed at all?

Larum: King, we must worship something. Furthermore,
Eternity in front of us extorts
The world-cry of the spirit, 'whither? whither?'
We are religious, and immortal soul
Turns to a fount immortal as itself.

Mammon:	But I deny your immortality:
	Immortal mayors, immortal aldermen!
	Think of the being you despise the most—
	Some jack-in-office, parasite or pimp:
	Would you have him immortal?—except in Hell?
	You see!—But you are earnest men: expound
	This new religion briefly.
Larum:	Tamberskelver,
	Our Head-inceptor, is our spokesman.
Mammon:	Speak,
	Head-inceptor Tamberskelver.
Tamberskelver:	King Mammon,
	Our confident appeal is dashed at once
	If you deny man's immortality.
	Our aspiration and our travail soar
	Aloft, and toil towards everlasting life
	For every individual soul of man.
Mammon:	And whence arose this confidence in me?
Tamberskelver:	You walked, deliberate, out of Christendom,
	The first of princes to disown the past.
Mammon:	That's the whole past, man's immortality:
	'Twas out of that I came.
Tamberskelver:	Have you not studied
	My treatises on soul?
Mammon:	I've never seen them.
Tamberskelver:	I sent them.—And my letters?
	Were they not read?
Mammon:	I never had your letters.
Tamberskelver:	They went unsigned. You would not know them
	mine.
Mammon:	A vagrant mass of anonymity from every land
	Followed me round the world.—You, Master
	Mayor, speak you. Your Tamberskelver
	Misses fire.
Larum:	But all I know I learnt from Tamberskelver.
Mammon:	That matters nothing: a foolish husband-man
	May sow a fertile plot; a bird, a wind

	Impregnate homely soil with brilliant flowers.
	Come, Master Mayor.
Larum:	My statement will be crude.
Mammon:	The better! I love all crudeness:
	Truth is crude.
Larum:	It's difficult.—On both sides of the Atlantic.
	Teutonic folk, and in the southern seas
	And lands afar, are ripe to have a god
	Of their own race: pubescence of the soul—
	That's our great phrase:—
Mammon:	Ah! Tamberskelver's?
Larum:	Yes.

This spiritual puberty of ours
Will sow the Universe with God: it must
Beget a God, or waste the seed of soul
In worshipping dead gods—which is a sort
Of psychic sodomy. We of the north
From age to age, since Olaf set the cross up,
Continued this unnatural vice (like all
The rest of Christendom), protesting still
Against the lusciousness of incense; art
In the church—immoral music, coloured glass;
The prurience of confession; virgin-worship,
Saints, transubstantiation, and the pomp
Whereby the wretched Latin races make
A mistress of religion: (although I change
The metaphor I keep within the sphere
Of sex, for that's illuminative in things
Religious). A decent, necessary wife
Our worship was; but now she's dead, and
                              we,
A few determined burghers of Christianstadt,
Refuse to bake our bread in a cold oven.

Mammon:	Audacious!—What killed her, Master Mayor?
Larum:	Her womb

Prolapsed: that is to say—out of the Christian
Theory of creation the bottom fell;

	And when your theory of creation goes
	Your God goes.
Mammon:	Certain! I like you, Master Mayor.
Larum:	A foreign God, too, at the best, was ours—
	Jehovah, one and single once, but one
	And triple since, a kind of Cerberus.
	We're tired of that—all that: we're tired of it.
	And the long gestant Teuton vengeance, cognate
	With puberty of soul that swells our thought,
	Dethrones the decadent neo-Hebraism ·
	Which Christianity is, and with its new
	Cosmogony of uncreated worlds
	Begins to shape a non-creating God.
Mammon:	All this intrigues me. And this God of yours?
Larum:	That's Tamberskelver's great discovery. Gods
	Are racial; and as long as races are,
	We cannot have a world-god. Languages
	Are races: that's understood; blood's little; words
	Are most when gods are canvassed or incept.
Mammon:	Incept? Begetters of a God may risk
	Neologisms—Proceed!
Larum:	The gods of old
	Evolved unconsciously in racial speech,
	And are, in every cult, naive, human monsters
	Of incoherent and incongruous parts
	Miraculously knit. For the first time
	In the world's record, we of Christianstadt,
	Unworthy but resolved inceptors, start
	A god whose evolution shall be conscious:
	No world-god, but a god Teutonic, foe
	Of Latin races, Slavs and yellow men,
	Of negroes, Hebrews, every other folk
	A god whom we can worship, being ours,
	And only ours. We did our best to like
	The God converted negroes pray to, Celts,
	Italians, Spaniards—people we despise:
	But none of us could stomach it: a God

Common to all the world is too debased,
Too vulgar, too adulterous for us.
In days and nights of prayer we steeped our souls,
And blanched them clear of preconception—

Mammon: Yes, Master Mayor. I know enough now. Gods
Are at a discount: Tamberskelver's plan
Is proof and pudding of it. A machine-made God?
A fattened god—a *pâté de fois gras*
For overnice religious epicures!
An end of divination! If any sign
Were wanting that the day of gods is done,
'Tis just this scheme to grow one locally
Under a forcing-frame. What the world needs
Is change: it's tired—as tired as you and I
Of all the past. But he who speaks to you
Is change incarnate, operant and crowned;
And you shall hear to-day when I address
The states the word you wait for. I approve
Your earnestness, your courage, your direct
Intelligence, authentic characters.—
Our revolutionists now.

Tamberskelver: There must be God!
Teuton, we call him: Teuton, God of us!
Pubescent soul in every age and clime
Produces God—

Mammon: You think so since you must.
But who would worship Tamberskelver's God?
Try and unthink that, friend.

*Larum, Tamberskelver, and the other
Inceptors go out.*

Mammon: My rebels now,
My worthy enemies.

Florimond: They call themselves Reformers.
Worthy? No reform is worth a king's applause.

*Crawford, Vibbe, Jelke and the other
Reformers enter.*

Mammon:	He from the Isles—which is he?
Crawford:	I, King Mammon.
Mammon:	Why did you leave your country?
Crawford:	Because reform is automatic there:
	Nothing can drive it on, nothing delay:
	The caucuses between them grind it out;
	Upper or nether stone alternately,
	According as the surly islanders
	Abuse their power and change the thing at will.
	In Thule we expect catastrophe.
Mammon:	And you're the man for that?
Crawford:	For action, King.
Mammon:	What do you want?
Crawford:	In our memorial, all
	Is well set out.
Mammon:	I haven't read it yet;
	Nor shall I.—Speak: What do you want, you five?
Crawford:	We want the Revolution.
Mammon:	State it, then.
	An end of kings, of course. And afterwards?
Crawford:	More than an end of kings. We want an end
	Of Lordship, titles, all gentility;
	We want an end of punishment, of crime;
	We want an end of service and respect;
	Of property and poverty; of war—
Mammon:	Yes, yes; an end of everything: I know;
	For when the king goes all goes at the last.
	What do you want begun?
Crawford:	We want the world
	Begun anew.
Mammon:	And so do I, and so
	Does every man. Having the world in hand,
	What follows?
Crawford:	Comfort follows first of all:
	Food, shelter, clothes for every being born,
	Insane or criminal, unfit or fit,

Idle or diligent—a corporate duty
That undertakes responsibility
In all relations: happiness itself,
For every human being as he is.

Mammon: What right have rascals to be happy?

Crawford: Right
And wrong are nothing: there they are, alive—
Desirous, envious, hungry, lustful men—
By no choice of their own.

Mammon: That I deny,
For men beget themselves; they are the passion
Of their parentage.—Well, after happiness
For every blessed body, what ensues?

Crawford: The breeding of a higher type of man.

Mammon: By what device?

Crawford: Unnatural selection:
I mean to say, by mating men and women
As horses are and cattle, poultry, dogs,
Instead of that old natural selection
By passionate love. Then, sterilizing fools,
Degenerates, weaklings, all who should not
                              breed.

Mammon: And what of happiness?

Crawford: Oh, folk may pair
And have the satisfaction of their senses
In barren beds by means well known to all!

Mammon: Most loathsome! What a hideous tyranny
Your world would be!—Why have you come
                           to me?

Crawford: We thought you were an anarch.

Mammon: An anarch? I?
The stark unchristened foe of anarchy!

Jelke: I take you for an evolutionist.
In our memorial you will find it said,
'The Christian times being past, there now
                         begins
The new Darwinian era.' We desire—

Mammon:	'Tis I shall give a title to the age.
	An evolutionist? No more than he
	Who makes religion serve him in the world
	May be pronounced a saint. This evolution,
	The errantry of nature, is known, is caught:
	Soon, tamed, apprenticed, disciplined and drilled,
	'Twill be our most obedient minister.
Vibbe:	But has our King no passion for the poor;
	No settled mind to dower disabled age;
	To ease the burden on the back of labour
	That every decade doubles; to provide
	An equal chance for every man; to draw
	The poison-fangs of bloated capital,
	That python gorged with proletary prey?
Mammon:	That python gorged with proletary prey!
	Park-eloquence, good friend. The world of men
	Is as an organism:—a python?—true;
	It sheds an annual slough of idlers, sots,
	Incompetents, degenerates, criminals;
	Or since the tissue of the macrocosm
	You call society is knit of men,
	As men are knit of divers plasmic cells,
	I take the failures for the excrement,
	The defecation of the commonwealth.
	In antique times such human garbage strewed
	With other ordure populous street, but now,
	Express as drainage in our more alert,
	More wholesome, more elaborate period, hides
	Our household refuse out of sight and mind,
	The hospital, asylum, poorhouse, jail,
	Sewers and cesspools of the social world,
	Relieve our towns of waste humanity,
	And keep the urban air as fresh as fresh.
Crawford:	But there must be no waste humanity!
Mammon:	No life then; only constipated death,
	A world by its own feculence undone.
Crawford:	Are we the feculence—

156

Mammon:	Dispose of waste
	Becomingly—ever more decently
	As knowledge grows; but have it out, and hence.
Crawford:	Are we the feculence of the world, Sir King?
Mammon:	You dabble in it. A traveller of the Isles,
	Your famous Gulliver, in Laputa found
	A yellow-faced projector up to the eyes
	In merd, pursuing the most ancient study
	Of all Laputan science, how to reduce
	The excrement of men to food again:
	A symbol of your socialists, who smear
	The proud and wealthy world with nastiness,
	Still fumbling at the emunctories of the state
	(I mean its economic processes)
	And churning up the stuff of the latrines
	(The broken men, the skilless and unskilled,
	The unemployed, the unemployable)
	In quest of menstruums to decoct from dung
	The sweetness of the rose, spindles to twist
	A silken fibre from putrescence, art
	And a cunning culture, a magic spell
	To rear in filth the unsown staff of life,
	To raise the dead and make perdition pay.
Crawford:	You slander men, King Mammon; the rich, the poor,
	The wise, the foolish, all are equal.
Mammon:	Yes?
	All men are equal. . . . You were going to say?
Crawford:	I was about to say, in the sight of God.
Mammon:	But not in yours?
Crawford:	No, not in any man's;
	Therefore we say, in God's.
Mammon:	Therefore you say
	In God's: that is, in Fairyland, in Heaven,
	In limbo, in Utopia—anywhere
	Save in this actual world of life and power!
	There is no other thing to say. I love

157

	Your honesty, and hope to make you mine;
	But not as Socialists—or Isocrats
	Of any breed. Isocracy: a rule
	Of all for all? Impossible while men
	Like Cæsar, like Napoleon, like myself,
	Are born into the world.
Crawford:	But we would have
	Us all Napoleon, King.
Mammon:	And if you had,
	Forthwith would come a greater than Napoleon.
	The world's magnificent; and plot by plot
	To turn it into routine on behalf
	Of weaker folk, incapable beyond
	A jog-trot use-and-wont, evaporates
	In presence of a monarch. Kill a whale
	With pin-pricks; whistle on a lion; catch
	A golden eagle in a spider's web!
	This socialism is mere misanthropy
	Erected to a creed; the evil smell
	Of Christendom, long dead and rotten, kept
	In salts and sponges to resuscitate
	The hopes of hungry malice; the fishy glow
	Upon the putrid carcass of religion—
Crawford:	Oh, King, oh, King, I cry red shame upon you!
Mammon:	Bold, and I need such comrades! None the less,
	The children of revulsion, of revolution—
	Communist, anarchist, nihilist—all these
	Are wriggling maggots in the fetid corpse
	Of Christendom: their sayings Jesus said—
	A futile message to a beaten race
	Under the heel of Rome; but not for us,
	The master people of the earth—nor yet
	For them, instinctive Jews that killed Him. I—
	You hear that word—I, Mammon, mean to make
	This mighty world a hundredfold itself.
	There shall be deeper depths of poverty,
	A more distressing toil, more warlike war,

158

An agony of spirit deadlier
Than that which drenched Gethsemane in blood;
A rapture of dominion hitherto
Unfelt by conquerors, kings or priests; a power,
A beauty and a glory of the world
Emerged from Christendom, like love's belov'd
With April from the wrinkled womb of death,
Delivered fresh to Aphrodite's arms.
The omnisolvent ether melt that image
For ever from my mind! My meaning hides
Behind the past like truth behind the veil
In Isis' temple.—I thank you, gentlemen,—
Or men, or fellow-men; you make me know
What I must say. Soon in St Olaf's Hall
I shall announce to Thule and the world
The very secret and the soul of me.
Await me there.—Our Neo-pagans now.

> *Crawford, Vibbe, Jelke and the other*
> *Reformers go out.*
> *Ribolt, Rolf and the Neo-Pagans enter, and*
> *prostrate themselves before Mammon.*

Mammon: What mummery is this? Rise; rise, I say!
No man must kneel to me. Though I am king
And absolute, the grosser adulation
Angers me.—Will you stand up, sirs! Florimond,
Are these men deaf?

Florimond: Not deaf, but mad, I think.

> *Ribolt, Rolf and the others raise their heads,*
> *but remain upon their knees.*

Mammon: A powerful face! Yes; You that look so strong.
Why do you kneel? You also are a man,
Of the same matter as the stars and me.

Ribolt: Hail, Baldur, Woden's son, and god of light.

Mammon: Fantastic man!

Ribolt: (*to Rolf and the others*) Did I not talk of this?

Rolf: You told how Baldur would not know himself.

Ribolt: I said it; and you see.—Unconscious God,
The fatal Norns who nightly haunt my pillow,
Command me to reveal to you your godhead,
Baldur, the winsomest, the most belov'd
Among immortals and the sons of men.
Behold the dreary twilight of the gods,
The twenty centuries of Christendom,
Expiring now, the golden age returns,
With you, our fairest god, to reign on earth
A thousand years. First of the Neo-pagans,
We kneel before you, desiring for ourselves
To be your priests, your guards, your ministers.

Mammon: How did your sect arise among the many
That gnaw the rotten bones of Christendom?

Ribolt: A fisherman, religious, old and wistful,
Bent on eternity far-seeing eyes
Of healthy age, and no asylum found,
No house, no harbour for a soul like his,
Salt as the sea and rough with storm and toil,
In any petty chapel-and-drawing-room
Apocalyptic Heaven of mother-church.
The saga of the north, in fragments known,
Beset his quickened mind: Hymir he loved
That splintered granite columns with his glance;
Woden and Thor, and Surtur of Muspelheim
Whose fervent sword set fire to the Universe,
When gods and giants met at Ragnarök.
But chief in fancy's aftermath there grew
A great uplifted vision of war-worn heroes
Winning Valhalla by a fiery death
When battle failed them.

Mammon: And did he? Did he?

Ribolt: What,
Oh, Baldur, god of light?

Mammon: This moves me, grips
Me firmly! Did he die like the old vikings,
Upon his funeral pyre sailing the sea?

Ribolt:	He died even so.
Mammon:	When was this greatness wrought?
Ribolt:	Last night, oh sinless one!
Mammon:	So men should die!

It shall become again a shameful thing
To wait in debile age, a pap-fed dotard
Shunning disdainful death. Men enter life
Unconscious, but the power accrues to leave it,
Hale, sane and self-possessed; therefore they
should.
My pagans, you are welcomest to me
Of all my folk. I feel how you became:
Such dreams I had in boyhood. I understand
Your thought of me as Baldur, and love you
well
For bringing me such beauty from the past,
Such elemental strength of the old time—
Which never yet was old, nor will be old!
But I am I, not Baldur: I am the king,
Greater than Baldur, greater than all the gods,
The first of men to be self-conscious. Man
Has come! The former cry was, or the hope,
The gods arrive, the heroes at their heels;
But I announce, at last, self-conscious man,
Greater than devil, angel, hero, god.

Ribolt: (*to Rolf and the others*) Baldur, or Mammon?
King or God?

Rolf: We want
A god again!

The Others: We want a god! a god!

Mammon: You shall have me. Await me in the hall.
Give them a special place that I may see them.

*Ribolt, Rolf and the others rise and go out,
accompanied by Florimond.*

Mammon: Why did I set them out? The madness!
Need

There is to be foolhardy in the things
That hap without inventing ambuscades
To trip and throttle us! I've made a morgue
Of Olaf's Hall! It seemed so great last night:—
And great it is; and I am fit for it.
If they should bleed! An ancient fallacy,
A Christian thing:—but they were Christians!—
                                        therefore
They'll bleed? Let them! And let them point at
                                        me,
And wink with sluggish lids and sightless eyes
As murdered folk were wont to do—in books!
I would be tested every way to learn
What limits shackle my material soul—
If there be limits to the power of one
Who knows himself unhuman.—Where am I
                                        now?
What mincemeat do I make? To argue out
A question like a Christian casuist doomed
For ever to eschew instinctive deeds!
I shame myself when not the utter shame
Of being ashamed should shame me. May it be
That I'm too young, and not adjusted yet
In mood and mind to my polarity?
'Twas in his thirtieth year the Son of Man
Began to turn the water into wine—
Napoleon's age when first he challenged fate
And leapt into the saddle of the world;
Mohammed knew the gauge of forty years
Before he set himself against mankind;
And Caesar, when he crossed the Rubicon,
Was old—an old, old man compared with me,
Who am not twenty-five. The Macedon?—
Yes, young and seminal, but sowing seed
At second-hand, a cultured person. I
Alone, since time began, bring with me news.
No mate I find among the mighty dead;

The greatest man of all the ages, youth
Commends me to my happy destiny:
No doubt perturbs me; prosperously I shall
Adjust the world's polarity to mine.

(Goes out)

(*from* The Triumph Of Mammon)

I am indeed your king, and greater: I
(Until the world, transmuted, understands
That men—that you, and she—are more than God,
As much as substance more than shadow is)
Shall be in Thule like a deity,
Inspiring, making, moulding greatness: greatness,
Which all your creeds have taught you to ascribe
To something not yourselves. Oh flesh and blood,
Oh gallant sex of men, sweet sex of women,
High hearts and brains of power, not anywhere
Is there a breath, a mote, that is not you!
I would I stood upon Mount Everest
And could be heard by every son of man!
The parasites that in our bodies burrow;
The lily and the rose whose passionate breath
Perfumes our love-thoughts with the scent of love;
The tawny brutes whose anguished roar appals
The desert and the jungle—they that suck
The steaming blood and tear the shuddering flesh
Of timid, browsing beasts; the timid beasts
Themselves; the birds that lace the summer winds
With music; houses, harvests, merchandise;
The woodland and the mountain and the sea;
The myriad suns that pave the Milky Way;
The furthest star, and all the stars of Heaven;
The vapours, metals, earths; their energies;
The lightning and the light; ethereal space:
All these—all that, is us, is you and me,
The conscience of the infinite Universe.
No supernatural thought must cloud your minds:
You have been told for twenty centuries
That that which is behind the Universe,
Its maker, God, or some obscurant will,
Transcends substantial things; and psychic powers,

Imagination, thought—the essences
Material of matter—have squandered craft
Enough to make another Universe
In building up nonentity, miscalled
The world of spirit! There is no such world:—
I speak to minds of every calibre,
And would be understood:—no spirit world;
No world but this, which is the Universe,
The whole, great, everlasting Universe.
And you are it—you, there, that sweep the streets,
You that make music, you that make the laws,
You that bear children, you that fade unloved.
Oh, if there be one here despised and mean,
Oppressed with self-contempt and cursed with fear,
I say to him:—Not anywhere at all
Is there a greater being than you—just you:
You are the lustre of a million suns—
The fuel of their fires, your flesh and blood;
And all the orbs that strew ethereal space
Are less than you, for you can feel, can know,
Can think, can comprehend the sum of things:
You are the infinite Universe itself
Become intelligent and capable.
Grasp it and hold it in your heart of hearts,
That nothing lies behind, nothing at all,
Except the ether woven from bourne to bourne—
If there be spatial bournes—continually
Evolving lightning, chrysosperm of space,
Electric lust for ever unconsumed,
Twisexed fertility that begets and breeds
The divers elements whereof we are,
And all the suns and all the galaxies:
Nothing of thought or oversoul behind,
About, above; but you and I in front,
The intellect, the passion and the dream,
The flower and perfume of the Universe.
You have been told for twenty centuries

That man upon a transient isthmus stands
Between the oceans of eternity;
And that the earth is but an academe
Where the poor human acolyte prepares
For joy in Heaven or penal fires of Hell,
Or here begins consecutive rebirths
That shall in other worlds perfection gain.
I say the earth itself is Heaven and Hell,
That every heart-beat is the crack of doom,
And every passing moment the judgment day;
That here and now we have eternity.
Time is not; never was: a juggling trick,
A very simple one, of three tossed balls,
The sun, the moon, the earth, to cheat our sense
With day and night and seasons of the year.
This is eternity: here once in space
The Universe is conscious in you and me;
And if the earth and all that is therein
Were now to end, the task, the pain, the woe,
The travail of the long millennial tides
Since life began, would like a pleasant fancy
Fade in the thoughtless memory of matter;
Because in me the infinite Universe
Achieves at last entire self-consciousness,
And could be well content to sleep again
For ever, still evolving in its sleep
Systems and constellations and tracts of suns.
But I would have you all even as I am!
I want you to begin a world with me,
Not for posterity, but for ourselves.
Prophets have told that there has seized on us
An agony of labour and design
For those that shall come after such as no age
Endured before. I, Mammon, tell you, No!
We have come after! We *are* posterity!
And time it is we had another world
Than this in which mankind excreted soul,

Sexless and used and immaterial,
Upon the very threshold of the sun,
To wonder why the earth should stink so! Men
Belov'd, women adored, my people, come,
Devise with me a world worth living in—
Not for our children and our children's children,
But for our own renown, our own delight!
All lofty minds, all pride, all arrogance,
All passion, all excess, all craft, all power,
All measureless imagination, come!
I am your King; come, make the world with me!

from

Mammon and His Message

[1908]

'MAMMON'S ARGUMENT'

(*from* Mammon And His Message)

Mammon tries to convert the aged Papal Legate Anselm to renounce Christianity and to follow him. Florimond is Mammon's Chancellor.

Mammon: This is the huge insanity of the world,
The time-old morbid mind that fears itself,
Unknowing and unknown. How great are men
To fashion out of ignorance and dread
Such greatness! For I know your spirit-world
Better than any prophet, poet, priest,
Philosopher, occultist, mystic, seer.
Hear me expound your dual universe:—
Man is a spirit, and his various life,
A bodying forth of the invisible;
The Universe and forms of time and space—
The garment and the symbolism of God;
The elements, the stars, earth and its brood—
The self-analysis, precipitation,
Pomp and deployment of the absolute:
The visible's the immaterial;
And only spirit's matter and momentous.
A noble Universe whose furthest nook
Is still a suburb of the City of God;
Where every star and every blade of grass,
Where every pulse and every thought reveals
The hallowed presence of divinity!

Anselm: You sin against the light knowing so well
What apparition matter is, and all
The Universe a mere similitude
And mutable appurtenance of God.

Mammon:	No God; no spirit; only matter. God?
	The cowardice of men flung forth to fill
	With welcome shadow an imagined void—
	Which never was, which by no chance can be.
	The unconscious ether fills the universe,
	Omnipotent, omniscient, omnipresent:
	No interstice in matter anywhere
	Even for the daintiest elf of other world;
	And in the infinite no interval
	To harbour alien immaterial dreams.
Anselm:	But spirit, God, may be material stuff,
	Of the same substance as the stars and us.
Mammon:	Not spirit, then; not God. You *know*!
Anselm:	I do.
	And may God pardon me my flash of sin!
Mammon:	Afraid of mystery men explained the unknown
	As something immaterial—spirit, God.
	But there's no mystery hidden in the unknown;
	There's nothing in the unknown; there's no
	unknown.
Anselm:	O King, the darkness! There the unknown hides!
Mammon:	Darkness?—negation; nil. Light?—wonder;
	woven
	Magnificence of seven mysterious stains,
	Ethereal substance of the Universe.
Anselm:	Bethink you, King; the silence of the night—
Mammon:	Silence that misanthropes have praised so, golden
	Against the silver sound of speech, is dull
	Inanity: the mystery of the whole resides
	In music—substance of the ether tuned
	To audible enchantment. Time's a lie,
	And space a trick. Eternity's the truth:
	Infinitude, the all-dynamic vast,
	Mystery of mysteries, known to any one,
	The everlasting durability
	Of the immeasurable universe;
	For all is matter, all is mystery, all

Is known: we are the universe become
Self-conscious; and nothing anywhere exists
Not us. All men are great, all men: unmade,
Incomparable, immeasurable, free—
The eternal Universe become self-conscious.
I'll have you understand this here and now,
Accept its truth and change the world with
                                            me.
My patience ends: I bring the greatest news;
I'll have it welcomed. We ourselves are fate;
We are the universe; we are all that is:
Outside of us nothing that is not us
Can be at all. No room! The universe
Is full of us, the matter of the stars;
The all-pervading ether seen as light,
Elaborate purity of rainbows; heard
As music, woven of elemental sounds;
And smelt in perfume, the poetry of flowers
Exhaled from sex, which in all plants and
                                        beasts
Secretes and sows the ethereal universe.
Seen in the light, in music heard, and smelt
In subtle odour of a thousand flowers,
In us the ether consciously becomes
Imagination, thought, religion, art.
We are the ether, we are the universe,
We are eternity: not sense, not spirit,
But matter; but the whole become self-conscious.
Whatever Heaven there is, whatever Hell,
Here now we have it; and I cannot wait
On God, the nothing, and his damned event
That mocked the world for sixty centuries;
Nor will I linger eating out my heart
While this new proxy of divinity
Your specious evolution, blunders on
From tedious age to age. I'll carve the world
In my own image, I, the first of men

To comprehend the greatness of mankind;
I'll melt the earth and cast it in my mould,
The form and beauty of the universe.
Say after me 'Get thee behind me, God;
I follow Mammon.' Say it, say it!

Anselm: God
Is God, eternal and unchangeable,
The God of my salvation.

Mammon: (*seizes Anselm by the throat*)
                                              Hideous liar,
Abominably old and impotent!
You know there is no God, no soul at all,
But only matter, ether polarised,
Condensed and shown and felt and understood,
Beholding, feeling, thinking, comprehending,
The subject-object of the Universe.
'Get thee behind me, God; I follow Mammon.'
Say it, before I fling you at my feet,
Abhorred senility, and stubborn past
Of the world! Say it, antiquity!

Anselm: Release
Me, King.

          (*Mammon flings Anselm from him violently.
          Anselm staggers and falls with a loud cry.*)

Mammon: Old craven heart of man, from truth
Divorced, God's creature, famulus and fool,
Go back to Rome and tell the triple-crown—

Florimond: (*who has entered quickly and is kneeling beside
                                              Anselm*)
He'll ne'er see Rome again: the legate's dead.

Mammon: Dead! Anselm dead! How dead?
Dead in the spirit—
Like all the world to all material truth,
Senseless and dead.

Florimond: Dead as a carcase, King.
How quickly he grows cold!

174

Mammon:　　　　　　　　Why should he die?
　　　　　　A wine-glass falls and breaks. Is human stuff
　　　　　　As brittle? Come; help him to his feet.
Florimond:　The man is dead. His heart: to-day the world
　　　　　　Trembles with broken hearts; the pace of life
　　　　　　Exceeds our staying power.

'THE DEATH OF GOD'

From a balcony Mammon quells the mob who have risen against him under Duke Oswald, as a result of the king's war against Christianity.

Mammon: Wolfhart, your guns
          Against these babbling windows and against
          The bawlers in the streets.

> (*Pause. Commands are heard; the movement of troops and shifting of artillery.*)

                                         If once again
          A voice is raised while I address you, fire.

Mammon: (*to Guendolen*) Oswald's no coward; but he
                                    cannot lead.—
                              (*Leaning over the balcony*)
          To men I know; who love me and whom I
                                         love:—
          Of Zenghis, of Tamerlane, of Attila,
          A casual echo haunts the cloistered mind;
          But Mahomet, triumphant still, usurps
          The hearts and souls of many millions, folk
          Profound in thought and dutiful in deed:
          Those other conquerors only scourged the world;
          The Arab prophet with the future fed
          The minds of men, and fledged the wings of hope
          With heaven and hell, the only destiny
          Within his ken; he gave them all he had,
          And therefore lives to-day devoutly cherished,
          Although the whole he gave was but a sign.
          For time I offer you eternity,
          Presenting to the world the Universe;
          And having wiped it clean of Christendom
          Intend a new beginning. Many starts
          The world has had, but always old beginnings
          Derived and eked and patched from hackneyed
                                         creeds.

I start as if before me never a thought
Had crossed the brain of man. If Tamerlane
Began with sixty followers, Mahomet
With two or three, I, with the might of Thule
And such a passion of belief, so rapt
A vision of the Universe, so great
A consciousness of power as now imbue
My being and empanoply my will,
May heedfully attempt a purpose vast
As change itself, and more momentous, more
Achievable than any ever yet
Accomplished by crusader, outlaw, king,
Warrior or world-compeller; for the age
Awaits me and the ancient systems, dead
And empty, from my path like winnowed husks,
Will vanish. Everywhere in high revolt
Against an order fallen to chaos, men
Must welcome us and swell our avalanche,
That from the Arctic to the Middle sea
Between the gulf of storms and Volga's tide
Will utterly abolish Christendom.

> (*The belfry bursts asunder and comes down with
> a heavy noise; the bells in a stream of molten
> metal splash among the falling stones; a broad
> sheet of flame soars up; and a prolonged in-
> drawn sigh fills the square.*
> *Florimond, much dismayed, goes out.*)

Mammon: The beauty and the cleanliness of flame,
The justice and the purity of war:
With these to purge the world of Christendom
And clear a space profane, that men at last
May be themselves, the conscious Universe!
Who asks a higher task, a nobler game,
A more heroic agony? Behold
Our beacon blazing—

> (*A soldier speaks indistinctly.*)

Mammon:	What?
The Soldier:	The fiery cross!
Mammon:	The fiery cross? The image pleases me:—

City to city, land to land shall speed
The message of deliverance, nightly flung
In brindled flame against the firmament,
As burning belfries topple into heaps
Resoldered by their molten chimes, and all
Cathedrals, churches, abbeys, purified
By fire, to dust and ashes crumble down,
Till not a consecrated stone shall stand
Upon another, and the smelted earth
Return to unadulterate matter free
From immaterial dreams that rot the air!

Gottlieb: The word of God! The word of God remains.
Wolfhart: The middle window; in the third story; there.—
Now, gunner—

Mammon: Do not fire! I pardon that.—
The word of God became a feeble lie
When men perceived how systems, suns and stars,
The earth and flowers and beasts and folk evolved
From the one staple of the Universe.
Bibles and liturgies are impotent;
In Baalbec who worships now the sun,
Or who in Zion to Jehovah pours
The first-born blood? The fanes are ruined; spent
The adoration that was only fond
Expedient, frantic makeshift for delayed
Self-consciousness in men; the truest creed
Dies like a mollusc when you crack the shell.
Instead of temples I bring the universe;
Instead of creeds I offer you yourselves,
The greatness of the universe become
Self-conscious; and I bid you welcome war—
My soldiers, trained to fight!—welcome a war
The noblest ever waged! Scope shall be yours
Such as ensanguined paladins enjoyed

178

Before our congresses decided *not*
To kill too many or to hurt too much.
The wealth of Christendom is there to seize,
And beauty waits on rapture and the sword.
We mean by war all that war ever meant.
Destruction's ministers, death's freemen, lust's
Exponent's daily like a blood-red dawn
In flames and crimson seas we shall advance
Against the ancient immaterial reign
Of spirit, and our watchword shall be still,
'Get thee behind me, God; I follow Mammon.'
And last, my comrades in this holiest war,
That you may know you are no common
          soldiers,
Tomorrow as a largess and free gift
From me, and as a token of your high
Vocation, each of you shall in gold receive
Ten sovereigns, earnest of the wealth and power,
The greatness that the lowliest may attain
On Mammon's battlefields.

The Soldiers: God save the King!
Mammon: God—save—the—King!

(*The Mob laughs loud, long and discordantly.*)

Mammon: Soldiers, that old inane
Accustomed cry must cease. God never saved
A king:—which king of all the catalogue
Who came to violent ends was saved by God,
From poison, from assassins, from the scaffold?
They died the death their enemies decreed.
God never yet did anything at all.
And why? Because there is none; never was.
Yet must our battle-cry be as I said,
'Get thee behind me, God; I follow Mammon.'
By God you understand the modern world,
A sink and overflow of decadence
With slimy rags and greasy fragments stopped:—

I mean that old fatigued philosophemes,
Deflowered religions, gelded poetries,
Frequent the markets, haunt the minds of men;
That rancid odds and ends of broken thought
Still gag conceit and stifle fantasy
To dupe the ambitious hunger of the age.
By Mammon you must understand a world
Purged of the fæcal past; a clean-run world;
A world begun again and wholly cured
Of God and sin, the immaterial wound
That pierces through and through, the open sore
That *is* not, though its grisly hue of death
Can frustrate vision, and its putrid stench
Envenom all the spaces of the air.
By Mammon you must understand a world
Where men are great and conscious of their
   greatness—
The very meanest intimately sure
That he himself is the whole universe
Become intelligent and capable.
Therefore our watchword and our battle-cry
Shall be henceforth—and let me hear it now—
'Get thee behind me, God; I follow Mammon.'

from

Fleet Street and Other Poems

[1909]

THE CRYSTAL PALACE

CONTRAPTION,—that's the bizarre, proper slang,
Eclectic word, for this portentous toy,
The flying-machine, that gyrates stiffly, arms
A-kimbo, so to say, and baskets slung
From every elbow, skating in the air.
Irreverent, we; but Tartars from Thibet
May deem Sir Hiram the Grandest Lama, deem
His volatile machinery best, and most
Magnific, rotatory engine, meant
For penitence and prayer combined, whereby
Petitioner as well as orison
Are spun about in space: a solemn rite
Before the portal of that fane unique,
Victorian temple of commercialism,
Our very own eighth wonder of the world,
The Crystal Palace.

                      So sublime! Like some
Immense crustacean's gannoid skeleton,
Unearthed, and cleansed, and polished! Were it so
Our paleontological respect
Would shield it from derision; but when a shed,
Intended for a palace, looks as like
The fossil of a giant myriapod! . . .
'Twas Isabey—sarcastic wretch!—who told
A young aspirant, studying tandem art
And medicine, that he certainly was born
To be a surgeon: 'When you try,' he said,
'To paint a boat you paint a tumour.'

Idea of its purpose, and no word
Can make your glass and iron beautiful.
Colossal ugliness may fascinate
If something be expressed; and time adopts
Ungainliest stone and brick and ruins them
To beauty; but a building lacking life,
A house that must not mellow or decay?—
'Tis nature's outcast. Moss and lichen? Stains
Of weather? From the first Nature said 'No!
Shine there unblessed, a witness of my scorn!
I love the ashlar and the well-baked clay;
My seasons can adorn them sumptuously:
But you shall stand rebuked till men ashamed,
Abhor you, and destroy you and repent!'

But come: here's crowd; here's mod; a gala day!
The walks are black with people: no one hastes;
They all pursue their purpose business-like—
The polo-ground, the cycle-track; but most
Invade the palace glumly once again.
It is 'again'; you feel it in the air—
Resigned habitués on every hand:
And yet agog; abandoned, yet concerned!
They can't tell why they come; they only know
They must shove through the holiday somehow.

In the main floor the fretful multitude
Circulates from the north nave to the south
Across the central transept—swish and tread
And murmur, like a seaboard's mingled sound.
About the sideshows eddies swirl and swing:
Distorting mirrors; waltzing-tops—wherein
Couples are wildly spun contrariwise
To your revolving platforms; biographs,
Or rifle-ranges; panoramas: choose!

As stupid as it was last holiday?
They think so,—every whit! Outside, perhaps?
A spice of danger in the flying-machine?
A few who passed that whirligig, their hopes
On higher things, return disconsolate
To try the Tartar's volant oratory.
Others again, no more anticipant
Of any active business in their own
Diversion, joining stalwart folk who sought
At once the polo-ground, the cycle-track,
Accept the ineludible; while some
(Insidious anti-climax here) frequent
The water-entertainments—shallops, chutes
And rivers subterrene:—thus, passive, all,
Like savages bewitched, submit at last
To be the dupes of pleasure, sadly gay—
Victims, and not companions, of delight!

Not all! The garden-terrace:—hark, behold,
Music and dancing! People by themselves
Attempting happiness! A box of reeds—
Accordion, concertina, seraphine—
And practised fingers charm advertent feet!
The girls can dance, but, O their heavy-shod
Unwieldy swains!—No matter:—hatless heads,
With hair undone, eyes shut and cheeks aglow
On blissful shoulders lie;—such solemn youths
Sustaining ravished donahs! Round they swing,
In time or out, but unashamed and all
Enchanted with the glory of the world.
And look! Among the laurels on the lawns
Torn coats and ragged skirts, starved faces flushed
With passion and with wonder!—hid away
Avowedly; but seen—and yet not seen!
None laugh; none point; none notice: multitude
Remembers and forgives; unwisest love
Is sacrosanct upon a holiday.

Out of the slums, into the open air
Let loose for once, their scant economies
Already spent, what was there left to do?
O sweetly, tenderly, devoutly think,
Shepherd and Shepherdess in Arcady!

A heavy shower; the Palace fills; begins
The business and the office of the day,
The eating and the drinking—only real
Enjoyment to be had, they tell you straight
Now that the shifty weather fails them too.
But what's the pother here, the blank dismay?
Money has lost its value at the bars:
Like tavern-tokens when the Boar's Head rang
With laughter and the Mermaid swam in wine,
Tickets are now the only currency.
Before the buffets, metal tables packed
As closely as mosaic, with peopled chairs
Cementing them, where damsels in and out
Attend with food, like disembodied things
That traverse rock as easily as air—
These are the havens, these the happy isles!
A dozen people fight for every seat—
Without a quarrel, unturbently: O,
A peaceable, a tame, a timorous crowd!
And yet relentless: this they know they need;
Here have they money's worth—some food, some drink;
And so alone, in couples, families, groups,
Consuming and consumed—for as they munch
Their victuals all their vitals ennui gnaws—
They sit and sit, and fain would sit it out
In tedious gormandize till firework-time.
But business beats them: those who sit must eat.
Tickets are purchased at besieged kiosks,
And when their value's spent—with such a grudge!—
They rise to buy again, and lose their seats;

For this is Mob, unhappy locust-swarm
Instinctive, apathetic, ravenous.

Beyond a doubt a most unhappy crowd!
Some scores of thousands searching up and down
The north nave and the south nave hungrily
For space to sit and rest to eat and drink:
Or captives in a labyrinth, or herds
Imprisoned in a vast arena; here
A moment clustered; there entangled; now
In reaches sped and now in whirlpools spun
With noises like the wind and like the sea,
But silent vocally: they hate to speak:
Crowd; Mob; a blur of faces featureless,
Of forms inane; a stranded shoal of folk

Astounding in the midst of this to meet
Voltaire, the man who worshipped first, who made
Indeed, the only god men reverence now,
Public Opinion. There he sits alert—
A cast of Houdon's smiling philosophe.
Old lion-fox, old tiger-ape—what names
They gave him!—better charactered by one
Who was his heir: 'The amiable and gay'.
So said the pessimist who called life sour
And drank it to the dregs. Enough: Voltaire—
About to speak: hands of a mummy clutch
The fauteuil's arms; he listens to the last
Before reply; one foot advanced; a new
Idea radiant in his wrinkled face.

Lunch in the grill-room for the well-to-do,
The spendthrifts and the connoisseurs of food—
Gourmet, gourmand, bezonian, epicure.
Reserved seats at the window?—Surely; you
And I must have the best place everywhere.
A deluge smudges out the landscape. Watch

The waiters since the scenery's not on view.
A harvest-day with them, our Switzers—knights
Of the napkin! How they balance loaded trays
And though they push each other spill no drop!
And how they glare at lazy lunchers, snatch
Unfinished plates sans 'by your leave', and fling
The next dish down, before the dazzled lout
(The Switzer knows his man) has time to con
The menu, every tip precisely gaged,
Precisely earned, no service thrown away.
Sign of an extra douceur, reprimand
Is welcomed, and the valetudinous
Voluptuary served devoutly: he
With cauteries on his cranium; dyed moustache;
Teeth like a sea-wolf's, each a work of art
Numbered and valued singly; copper skin;
And neither eyelids pouched:—why he alone
Is worth a half-day's wage! Waiters for him
Are pensioners of indigestion, paid
As secret criminals disburse blackmail,
As Attic gluttons sacrificed a cock
To Æsculapius to propitiate
Hygeia—if the classic flourish serves!

'Grilled soles?'—for us;—Kidneys to follow.—Now,
Your sole, sir; eat it with profound respect.
A little salt with one side;—scarce a pinch!
The other side with lemon;—tenderly!
Don't crush the starred bisection;—count the drops!
Those who begin with lemon miss the true
Aroma: quicken sense with salt, and then
The subtle, poignant, citric savour tunes
The delicate texture of the foam-white fish,
Evolving palatable harmony
That music might be happy chance express.
A crust of bread—(eat slowly: thirty chews,
Gladstonian rumination)—to change the key.

And now the wine—a well-decanted, choice
Château, *bon per*; a decade old; not more;
A velvet claret, piously unchilled.
A boiled potato with the kidney . . . No!
Barbarian! Vandal! Sauce? 'Twould ruin all!
The kidney's the potato's sauce. Perpend:
You taste the esoteric attribute
In food; and know that all necessity
Is beauty's essence. Fill your glass: salute
The memory of the happy neolith
Who had the luck to hit on roast and boiled.
Finish the claret.—Now the rain has gone
The clouds are winnowed by the sighing south,
And hidden sunbeams through a silver woof
A warp of pallid bronze in secret ply.

Cigars and coffee in the billiard-room.
No soul here save the marker, eating chops;
The waiter and the damsel at the bar,
In listless talk. A most uncanny thing,
To enter suddenly a desolate cave
Upon the margent of the sounding Mob!
A hundred thousand people, class and mass,
In and about the palace, and not a pair
To play a hundred up! The billiard-room's
The smoking-room; and spacious too, like all
The apartments of the Palace:—why
Unused on holidays? The marker: aged;
Short, broad, but of a presence; reticent
And self-respecting; not at all the type:—
'O well,' says he; 'the business of the room
Fluctuates very little, year in, year out.
My customers are seasons mostly.' One
On the instant enters: a curate, very much
At ease in Zion—and in Sydenham.
He tells two funny stories—not of the room;
And talks about the stage. 'In London now,'

He thinks, 'the play's the thing.' He undertakes
To entertain and not to preach: you see,
It's with the theatre and the music-hall,
Actor and artiste, the parson must compete.
Every bank-holiday and special day
The Crystal Palace sees him. Yes; he feels
His hand's upon the public pulse on such
Occasions. O, a sanguine clergyman!

Heard in the billiard-room the sound of Mob,
Occult and ominous, besets the mind:
Something gigantic, something terrible
Passes without; repasses; lingers; goes;
Returns and on the threshold pants in doubt
Whether to knock and enter, or burst the door
In hope of treasure and a living prey.
The vainest fantasy! Rejoin the crowd:
At once the sound depreciates. Up and down
The north nave and the south nave hastily
Some tens of thousands walk, silent and sad,
A most unhappy people.—Hereabout
Cellini's Perseus ought to be. Not that;
That's stucco—and Canova's: a stupid thing;
The face and posture of a governess—
A nursery governess who's had the nerve
To pick a dead mouse up. It used to stand
Beside the billiard-room, against the wall,
A cast of Benvenuto's masterpiece—
That came out lame, as he foretold, despite
His dinner dishes in the foundry flung.
They shift their sculpture here haphazard.—That?
King Francis—by Clesinger—on a horse.
Absurd: most mounted statues are.—And this?
Verrochio's Coleone. Not absurd:
Grotesque and strong, the battle-harlot rides
A stallion; fore and aft, his saddle, peaked
Like a mitre, grips him as in a vice.

In heavy armour mailed; his lifted helm
Reveals his dreadful look; his brows are drawn;
Four wrinkles deeply trench his muscular face;
His left arm half-extended, and the reins
Held carelessly, although the gesture's tense;
His right hand wields a sword invisible;
Remorseless pressure of his lips protrudes
His mouth; he would decapitate the world.

The light is artificial now; the place
Phantasmal like a beach in hell where souls
Are ground together by an unseen sea.
A dense throng in the central transept, wedged
So tightly they can neither clap nor stamp,
Shouting applause at something, goad themselves
In sheer despair to think it rather fine:
'We came here to enjoy ourselves. Bravo,
Then! Are we not?' Courageous folk beneath
The brows of Michael Angelo's Moses dance
A cakewalk in the dim Renascence Court.
Three people in the silent Reading-room
Regard us darkly as we enter: three
Come in with us, stare vacantly about,
Look from the window and withdraw at once.
A drama; a balloon; a Beauty Show:—
People have seen them doubtless; but none of those
Deluded myriads walking up and down
The north nave and the south have anxiously—
And aimlessly, so silent and so sad.

The day wears; twilight ends; the night comes down.
A ruddy targelike moon in a purple sky,
And the crowd waiting on the fireworks. Come:
Enough of Mob for one while. This way out—
Past Linacre and Chatham, the second Charles,
Venus and Victory—and Sir William Jones
In placid contemplation of a State!—
Down the long corridor to the district train.

'FOG'

(*from* The Feast of St Hilary)

I love the fog: in every street
  Shrill muffled cries and shapes forlorn,
The frosted hoof with stealthy beat,
  The hollow-sounding motor-horn:

A fog that lasts till, gently wrung
  By Pythian pangs, we realize
That Doomsday somewhere dawns among
  The systems and the galaxies,

And ruin at the swiftest rate
  The chartered destinies pursue;
While as for us, our final fate
  Already fixed with small ado,

Spills on our heads no wrathful cup,
  Nor wrecks us on a fiery shore,
But leaves us simply swallowed up
  In London fog for evermore.

THE TESTAMENT OF SIR SIMON SIMPLEX
CONCERNING AUTOMOBILISM

That railways are inadequate appears
Indubitable now. For sixty years
Their comfort grew until the *train de luxe*
Arrived, arousing in conducted Cook's,
And other wholesale, tourists, an envious smart,
For here they recognized the perfect art
And science of land-travel. Now we sing
A greater era, hail a happier Spring.
The motor-car reveals ineptitude
In railway-trains; and travellers conclude
The railway is archaic: strictly true,
Although the reason sounds as false as new:—
Railways are democratic, vulgar, laic;
And who can doubt Democracy's archaic?
The railway was the herald and the sign,
And powerful agent in the swift decline
Of Europe and the West. The future sage
Will blame sententiously the railway age,
Preachers upon its obvious vices pounce,
And poets, wits and journalists pronounce
The nineteenth century in prose and rhyme
The most unhappy period of time.
That nations towering once in pomp and pride
Of monarchs, rank and breeding, should subside
To one dead undistinguishable horde
Sans sceptre, mitre, coronet and sword,
Reverting to a pithecoidal state
May be the purpose of recurrent fate;
But that such folks should to themselves appear
Progressing toward a great millennial year
Is just the bitter-sweet, the chilly-hot,
The subtle metaphysic of the plot.

The last age saw the last stage of the fit
That pestered, when the Roman Empire split,
The catalytic centuries: the strange
Insanity that fed on secular change;
The general paralysis of men
That ended in the railway and the wen
Called London: from the Tiber to the Thames,
From dreaming empire to delirious aims
That move the laughter of the careless fates,
And effervesce in socialistic pates.

But convalescence with the car begins
And petrol expiates our railway sins.
Before we know we shall with joy behold
A world as sane as any world of old;
From labour and electoral problems free,
A world the fibre of whose health shall be,
No Will to be the Mob, but mastering all,
A Will to be the Individual;
For every Mob exhales a poisonous breath,
And Socialism is decadence, is death:
The Mob expropriates, degrades, destroys;
The Individual conquers, makes, enjoys.
Not till the motor was the contrast plain,
Because the separate classes of the train
Deceived us with a choice of company;
And, when he liked, the tame celebrity,
The genius, man of wealth, aristocrat,
By means of tips through any journey sat
In cornered state; or with sufficient pelf
Could purchase a compartment for himself.
He rather would have deemed himself a snob
Than that the train could turn him into Mob,
Till automotion's privacy and pride
Exposed the grossness of the railway ride;
For 'twas the freedom of the motor-car
That showed how tyrannous the railways are.

To go by train from one place to another
You have to brave the station's smoke and smother:
The train derides you there; 'twill never come
To pick you up, nor turn, to see you home,
A single wheel; the getting under way,
The true vexation of a holiday,
The stolid train permits you to deplore;
But with your automobile at the door—
Why, there you are, nor need you stir a foot,
Man and portmanteau instantly *en route*!
You buy a ticket if you go by train
At some offensive loophole, which you gain
After prolonged attendance in a queue—
Whatever class you take, a motley crew:
And to await one's turn, like patient Job,
Unites one with a vengeance to the Mob.
Then you may miss the train; but *you* must wait
Its advent and departure prompt or late.
The motor soothes, the railway racks, your nerves;
The train commands, the automobile serves.
The automobile nurses all caprice,
And gives the longest life a second lease;
Indulges indolence, and even in me
Increases individuality.
I thought and many my opinion shared
That the deceased politic who declared
That all were Socialists, had told, perhaps,
A fib, exploited in a studied lapse
Of platform declamation as a sop
To catch erratic voters on the hop,
The strained politeness of a caustic mind,
A dead-lift effort to say something kind.
'Twas more than that: not only had we learned
To suffer Socialism; our souls discerned
A something fine about it; egoists even
Perceived therein at last a mundane heaven.

'Life is a railway journey', genius thought—
(The erring genius very cheaply bought
With gilded apples of Asphaltites)—
'Thieves bearing swag, and poets sprouting bays,
The ring, the cabinet, scortatory dames,
Bishops, sectarians of a myriad names,
Bankers and brokers, merchants, mendicants,
Booked in the same train like a swarm of ants;
First, second, third, class, mass and mob expressed
Together to the Islands of the Blest—
Each passenger provided with a groat
To pass the Stygian stile for Charon's boat.
Or broad or narrow as the gauge may run,
None leaves the track without disaster; none
Escapes a single stoppage on the way;
And none arrives before his neighbour may.
In the guard's van my sacred luggage knocks
Against the tourist's traps, the bagman's box;
And people with inferior aims to mine
Partake the rapid transit of the line.
But this is culture of the social school,
And teaches me to lead my life by rule
Empirical, of positive descent
And altruistic self-embezzlement.
Life *is* a railway journey: I rejoice
That folk whose purpose, visage, clothes and voice
Offend me will continue to offend
In the same train until the journey's end.'

So spoke the genius in pathetic rage.—
The socialistic and the railway age
Were certainly coeval; machinery too
Equated communism; and every new
Development of electricity
Was welcomed by the Mob with three times three,
Convinced the world at last was through the wood—
Right through to Universal Brotherhood!

Conceive it:—Universal Brotherhood,
With everybody feeble, kind and good!
I, even I, Sir Simon Simplex, know
The world would end to-day if that were so.
What spur does man require, what stinging zest
To do still better than his level best?
Why, enemies; and if he has them not
He must unearth and beat them till they're hot;
For only enmity can train and trounce
The cortex and the muscle to an ounce.
Let Socialists deny, mistaking peace,
That only with the world will warfare cease;
When *we* beheld the battle-flags unfurled
We know the fates phlebotomize the world,
And alternate with peace's patent pill,
The old heroic cure for every ill.

Life was a railway journey; foe and friend,
Infected with nostalgy of the end,
Awaited patiently the crack of doom;
But thank the powers that be, the motor boom,
Predestined to postpone the judgment-day,
Arrived in time to show a better way.
And when the automobile came we found
Our incorrupt opinion safe and sound,
Inoculated only by the schism,
For ever proof against all Socialism.
The motor stops the decadence: not all
Are in the same train with the prodigal,
The Christian scientist, the *souteneur*,
The Gothamite, the man from anywhere,
Domestic Gill and idiomatic Jack,
The wheedling knave, the sneak, the hectoring quack;
The man of broader mind and farther goal
Is not entrained with Lubin Littlesoul;
Your gentleman by birth with quickened sense,
Refined requirements and abundant pence,

And men of faculty and swelling aim
Who conquer riches, power, position, fame,
Are not entrained with loafers, quibblers, cranks,
Nor with the Mob who never leave the ranks,
With plodding dullness, unambitious ease,
And discontented incapacities.

Goodwill is in the blood, in you and me,
And most in men of wealth and pedigree;
So rich and poor, men, women, age and youth
Imagined some ingredient of truth
In Socialistic faith that there could be
A common basis of equality.
But now we know and by the motor swear
The prepossession was as false as fair;
Men are not equal; no two intellects
Are of a calibre; desires, defects,
Powers, aptitudes, are never on a par,
No more than finger-prints and noses are.
And on my soul and conscience I maintain
Political equality's as vain
As personal: for instance, I would place
The franchise on a principle of race,
And give the Saxon's forward reach a felt
Prepotence o'er the backward-glancing Celt;
And if his chauffeur counts as one, why then
Sir Simon Simplex should be reckoned ten.
I call Democracy archaic, just
As manhood suffrage is atavic lust
For folkmotes of the prime, whose analogue
In travel was the train, a passing vogue:
The automobile put an end to that,
And left Democracy as fallen and flat
As railway-stock. Wealth and the crafty hand
That gathers wealth had always at command
Horse-carriages for private travel, but
The pace had got beyond that leisured rut;

Class, mass and mob for fifty years and more
Had all to travel in the jangling roar
Of railways, the nomadic caravan
That stifled individual mind in man,
Till automobilism arose at last!
Now with the splendid periods of the past
Our youthful century is proudly linked;
And things that Socialism supposed extinct,
Degree, nobility and noble strife,
A form, a style, a privacy in life
Will reappear; and, crowning nature's plan,
The individual and the gentleman
In England reassume his lawful place
And vindicate the greatness of the race.

ST MICHAEL'S MOUNT

St Michael's Mount, the tidal isle,
  In May with daffodils and lilies
Is kirtled gorgeously a while
  As ne'er another English hill is:
About the precipices cling
The rich renascence robes of Spring.

Her gold and silver, nature's gifts,
  The prodigal with both hands showers:
O not in patches, not in drifts
  But round and round, a mount of flowers—
Of lilies and of daffodils,
The envy of all other hills.

And on the lofty summit looms
  The castle: none could build or plan it.
The foursquare foliage springs and blooms,
  The piled elaborate flower of granite,
That not the sun can wither; no,
Nor any tempest overthrow.

THE WASP

Once as I went by rail to Epping Street,
Both windows being open, a wasp flew in;
Through the compartment swung and almost out
Scarce seen, scarce heard; but dead against the pane
Entitled 'Smoking', did the train's career
Arrest her passage. Such a wonderful
Impervious transparency, before
That palpitating moment, had never yet
Her airy voyage thwarted. Undismayed,
With diligence incomparable, she sought
An exit, till the letters like a snare
Entangled her; or else the frosted glass
And signature indelible appeared
The key to all the mystery: there she groped,
And flirted petulant wings, and fiercely sang
A counter-spell against the sorcery,
The sheer enchantment that inhibited
Her access to the world—her birthright there!
So visible, and so beyond her reach!
Baffled and raging like a tragic queen,
She left at last the stencilled tablet; roamed
The pane a while to cool her regal ire,
Then tentatively touched the window-frame:
Sure footing still, though rougher than the glass;
Dissimilar in texture, and so obscure!

Perplexed now by opacity with foot and wing
She coasted up and down the wood and worked
Her wrath to passion-point again. Then from the frame
She slipped by chance into the open space
Left by the lowered sash:—the world once more
In sight! She paused; she closed her wings, and felt
The air with learned antennæ for the smooth
Resistance that she knew now must belong

To such mysterious transparences.
No foothold? Down she fell—six inches down!—
Hovered a second, dazed and dubious still;
Then soared away a captive queen set free.

THE THAMES EMBANKMENT
(*from* Rail and Road)

As gray and dank as dust and ashes slaked
With wash of urban tides the morning lowered;
But over Chelsea Bridge the sagging sky
Had colour in it—blots of faintest bronze,
The stains of daybreak. Westward slabs of light
From vapour disentangled, sparsely glazed
The panelled firmament; but vapour held
The morning captive in the smoky east.
At lowest ebb the tide on either bank
Laid bare the fat mud of the Thames, all pinched
And scalloped thick with dwarfish surges. Cranes,
Derricks and chimney-stalks of the Surrey-side,
Inverted shadows, in the motionless,
Dull, leaden mirror of the channel hung:
Black flags of smoke broke out, and in the dead
Sheen of the water hovered underneath,
As in the upper region, listlessly,
Across the viaduct trailing plumes of steam,
The trains clanked in and out.

                       Slowly the sun
Undid the homespun swathing of the clouds,
And splashed his image on the northern shore—
A thing extravagantly beautiful:
The glistening, close-grained canvas of the mud
Like hammered copper shone, and all about
The burning centre of the mirror'd orbs
Illimitable depth of silver fire
Harmonious beams the overtones of light,
Suffused the emboss'd, metallic river bank.
Woven of rainbows a dewdrop can dissolve
And packed with power a simple lens can wield,
The perfect, only source of beauty, light

Reforms uncouthest shapelessness and turns
Decoloured refuse into ornament;
The leafless trees that lined the vacant street
Had all their stems picked out in golden scales,
Their branches carved in ebony; and shed
Around them by the sanction of the morn
In lieu of leaves each wore an aureole.

Barges at anchor, barges stranded, hulks
Ungainly, in the unshorn beams and rich
Replenished planet of a winter sun,
Appeared ethereal, and about to glide
On high adventure chartered, swift away
For regions undiscovered.

                    Huddled wharfs
A while, and then once more a reach of Thames
Visibly flowing where the sun and wind
Together caught the current. Quays and piers
To Vauxhall Bridge, and there the Baltic Wharf
Exhibited its wonders: figureheads
Of the old wooden walls on gate and post—
Colossal torsos, bulky bosoms thrown
Against the storm, sublime uplifted eyes
Telling the stars. As white as ghosts
They overhung the way, usurping time
With carved memorials of the past. Forlorn
Elysium of the might of England!

                      Gulls,
Riparian scavengers, arose and wheeled
About my head, for morsels begging loud
With savage cries that piercingly reverbed
The tempest's dissonance. Birds in themselves
Unmusical and uninventive ape
Impressive things with mocking undesigned:
The eagle's bark mimics the crashing noise

That shakes his eyry when the thunder roars;
And chanticleer's imperious trumpet-call
Re-echoes round the world his ancestor's
Barbaric high-wrought challenge to the dawn;
But birds of homely feather and tuneful throat,
With music in themselves and masterdom,
To beauty turn obsessive sight and sound:
The mounting larks, compact of joyful fire,
Render the coloured sunlight into song;
Adventurous and impassioned nightingales
Transmute the stormy equinox they breast
With courage high, for hawthorn thickets bound
When spring arrives, into the melody
That floods the forest aisles; the robin draws
Miraculously from the rippling brook
The red wine of his lay; blackbird and thrush,
Prime-artists of the woodland, proudly take
All things sonorous for their province, weave
The gold-veined thunder and the crystal showers,
The winds, the rivers and the choir of birds
In the rich strains of their chromatic score.

By magic mechanism the weltering clouds
Re-grouped themselves in continents and isles
That diapered the azure firmament;
And sombre chains of cumulus, outlined
In ruddy shade along the house-tops loomed,
Phantasmal alp on alp. The sunbeams span
Chaotic vapour into cosmic forms,
And juggled in the sky, with hoods of cloud
As jesters twirl on sticks their booby-caps—
The potent sunbeams, that had fished the whole
Enormous mass of moisture from the sea,
Kneaded, divided and divided, wrought
And turned it to a thousand fantasies
Upon the ancient potter's wheel, the earth.

An ashen canopy of cloud,
The dense immobled sky, high-pitched above
The wind's terrestrial office, overhung
The city when the morning train drew out.
Leaping along the land from town to town,
Its iron lungs respired its breath of steam,
Its resonant flanges, and its vertebral
Loose-jointed carcase of a centipede
Gigantic, hugged and ground the parallel
Adjusted metals of its destined way
With apathetic fatalism, the mark
Of all machinery.—From Paddington
To Basingstoke the world seemed standing still;
Nothing astir between the firmaments
Except the aimless tumult of the wind,
And clanging travail of the ponderous train
In labour with its journey on the smooth,
The ineludible, the shining rails.

SNOW

I

'Who affirms that crystals are alive?'
    I affirm it, let who will deny:—
Crystals are engendered, wax and thrive,
    Wane and wither; I have seen them die.

Trust me, masters, crystals have their day,
    Eager to attain the perfect norm,
Lit with purpose, potent to display
    Facet, angle, colour, beauty, form.

II

Water-crystals need for flower and root
    Sixty clear degrees, no less, no more;
Snow, so fickle, still in this acute
    Angle thinks, and learns no other lore:

Such its life, and such its pleasure is,
    Such its art and traffic, such its gain,
Evermore in new conjunctions this
    Admirable angle to maintain.

Crystalcraft in every flower and flake
    Snow exhibits, of the welkin free:
Crystalline are crystals for the sake,
    All and singular, of crystalry.

Yet does every crystal of the snow
    Individualize, a seedling sown
Broadcast, but instinct with power to grow
    Beautiful in beauty of its own.

Every flake with all its prongs and dints
　　Burns ecstatic as a new-lit star:
Men are not more diverse, finger-prints
　　More dissimilar than snow-flakes are.

Worlds of men and snow endure, increase,
　　Woven of power and passion to defy
Time and travail: only races cease,
　　Individual men and crystals die.

III

Jewelled shapes of snow whose feathery showers,
　　Fallen or falling wither at a breath,
All afraid are they, and loth as flowers
　　Beasts and men to tread the way to death.

Once I saw upon an object-glass,
　　Martyred underneath a microscope,
One elaborate snow-flake slowly pass,
　　Dying hard, beyond the reach of hope.

Still from shape to shape the crystal changed,
　　Writhing in its agony; and still,
Less and less elaborate, arranged
　　Potently the angle of its will.

Tortured to a simple final form,
　　Angles six and six divergent beams,
Lo, in death it touched the perfect norm
　　Verifying all its crystal dreams!

IV

Such the noble tragedy of one
　　Martyred snow-flake. Who can tell the fate
Heinous and uncouth of showers undone,
　　Fallen in cities!—showers that expiate

Errant lives from polar worlds adrift
  Where the great millennial snows abide;
Castaways from mountain-chains that lift
  Snowy summits in perennial pride;

Nomad snows, or snows in evil day
  Born to urban ruin, to be tossed,
Trampled, shovelled, ploughed and swept away
  Down the seething sewers: all the frost

Flowers of heaven melted up with lees,
  Offal, recrement, but every flake
Showing to the last in fixed degrees
  Perfect crystals for the crystal's sake.

                    V

Usefulness of snow is but a chance
  Here in temperate climes with winter sent,
Sheltering earth's prolonged hibernal trance:
  All utility is accident.

Sixty clear degrees the joyful snow,
  Practising economy of means,
Fashions endless beauty in, and so
  Glorifies the universe with scenes

Arctic and antarctic: stainless shrouds,
  Ermine woven in silvery frost, attire
Peaks in every land among the clouds
  Crowned with snows to catch the morning's fire.

from

The Testament of John Davidson

[1908]

'THE LAST JOURNEY'

(*from* The Testament Of John Davidson)

I felt the world a-spinning on its nave,
  I felt it sheering blindly round the sun;
I felt the time had come to find a grave:
  I knew it in my heart my days were done.
I took my staff in hand; I took the road,
And wandered out to seek my last abode.
      Hearts of gold and hearts of lead
        Sing it yet in sun and rain,
      'Heel and toe from dawn to dusk,
      Round the world and home again.'

O long before the bere was steeped for malt,
  And long before the grape was crushed for wine,
The glory of the march without a halt,
  The triumph of a stride like yours and mine
Was known to folk like us, who walked about,
To be the sprightliest cordial out and out!
      Folk like us, with hearts that beat,
        Sang it too in sun and rain—
      'Heel and toe from dawn to dusk,
      Round the world and home again.'

My feet are heavy now, but on I go,
  My head erect beneath the tragic years.
The way is steep, but I would have it so;
  And dusty, but I lay the dust with tears,
Though none can see me weep: alone I climb
The rugged path that leads me out of time—

Out of time and out of all,
   Singing yet in sun and rain,
'Heel and toe from dawn to dusk,
Round the world and home again.'

Farewell the hope that mocked, farewell despair
   That went before me still and made the pace.
The earth is full of graves, and mine was there
   Before my life began, my resting-place;
And I shall find it out and with the dead
Lie down for ever, all my sayings said—
   Deeds all done and songs all sung,
     While others chant in sun and rain,
   'Heel and toe from dawn to dusk,
   Round the world and home again.'

Bibliography of
John Davidson's Work

POEMS

Diabolus Amans. A Dramatic Poem. Glasgow, 1885.
In a Music-Hall, and Other Poems. 1891.
Fleet Street Eclogues. Two series, 1893 and 1896.
Ballads and Songs. 1894.
St. George's Day: A Fleet Street Eclogue. New York, 1895. Included in second series later.
New Ballads. 1897.
The Last Ballad. 1899.
The Testament of a Vivisector. 1901.
The Testament of a Man Forbid. 1901.
The Testament of an Empire-Builder. 1902.
The Testament of a Prime Minister. 1904.
The Ballad of a Nun. 1905.
Selected Poems. 1905.
Holiday, and Other Poems. 1906.
The Testament of John Davidson. 1908.
Fleet Street, and Other Poems. 1909.

DRAMATIC WORKS

Bruce. Glasgow, 1886.
Smith. A Tragedy. Glasgow, 1888.
Plays. Greenock, 1889. (1st Edition, 1st Issue, containing: An Unhistorical Pastoral, A Romantic Farce, and Scaramouch in Naxos.)
Scaramouch in Naxos. 1890. (1st Edition, 2nd Issue, of above sheets transferred to T. Fisher Unwin in London.)

Scaramouch in Naxos. 1893. (1st Edition, 3rd Issue, with addition of Elkin Mathews' and Lane's title-page.)

Plays. 1894. (2nd Edition. Reprint of the above, with the addition of *Bruce* and *Smith*. Frontispiece by Beardsley.)

Godfrida. 1898.

Self's the Man. 1901.

The Knight of the Maypole. 1903.

The Theatrocrat. 1905.

God and Mammon: The Triumph of Mammon. 1907.

God and Mammon: Mammon and his Message. 1908.

FICTION

The North Wall. 1885.

Perfervid: the Career of Ninian Jamieson. 1890.

The Great Men and A Practical Novelist. 1891.

Laura Ruthven's Widowhood. 1892. (In collaboration with C. J. Wills.)

Baptist Lake. 1894.

A Full and True Account of the Wonderful Mission of Earl Lavender. 1895.

Miss Armstrong's and Other Circumstances. 1896.

MISCELLANEOUS WRITINGS AND TRANSLATIONS

Persian Letters. 1892. (A translation from Montesquieu, with a Memoir of the Author.)

Sentences and Paragraphs. 1893.

A Random Itinerary. 1894.

For the Crown. 1896. (A translation from Coppée. The libretto of *The Cross and the Crescent*, an opera by Colin McAlpin founded on Davidson's *For the Crown*, was published in 1903, the year of its production by the Moody Manners Opera Company Limited.)

A Rosary. 1903.

A Queen's Romance. 1904. (A version of Hugo's *Ruy Blas*.)

———

Davidson selected passages in prose and verse for Birket Foster's *Pictures of Rustic Landscape* (1896), and wrote an Introduction to Volume XXXVIII, the Sonnets, for Sydney Lee's *The Complete Works of William Shakespeare*. New York, 1909.

Index

217

218

219